Polar Bear

Animal
Series editor: Jonathan Burt

Already published

Albatross Graham Barwell · *Ant* Charlotte Sleigh · *Ape* John Sorenson · *Badger* Daniel Heath Justice
Bat Tessa Laird · *Bear* Robert E. Bieder · *Beaver* Rachel Poliquin · *Bedbug* Klaus Reinhardt
Bee Claire Preston · *Beetle* Adam Dodd · *Bison* Desmond Morris · *Camel* Robert Irwin
Cat Katharine M. Rogers · *Chicken* Annie Potts · *Cockroach* Marion Copeland · *Cow* Hannah Velten
Crocodile Dan Wylie · *Crow* Boria Sax · *Deer* John Fletcher · *Dog* Susan McHugh · *Dolphin* Alan Rauch
Donkey Jill Bough · *Duck* Victoria de Rijke · *Eagle* Janine Rogers · *Eel* Richard Schweid
Elephant Dan Wylie · *Falcon* Helen Macdonald · *Flamingo* Caitlin R. Kight · *Fly* Steven Connor
Fox Martin Wallen · *Frog* Charlotte Sleigh · *Giraffe* Edgar Williams · *Goat* Joy Hinson
Goldfish Anna Marie Roos · *Gorilla* Ted Gott and Kathryn Weir · *Guinea Pig* Dorothy Yamamoto
Hare Simon Carnell · *Hedgehog* Hugh Warwick · *Hippopotamus* Edgar Williams · *Horse* Elaine Walker
Hyena Mikita Brottman · *Kangaroo* John Simons · *Kingfisher* Ildiko Szabo · *Leech* Robert G. W. Kirk
and Neil Pemberton · *Leopard* Desmond Morris · *Lion* Deirdre Jackson · *Lizard* Boria Sax
Llama Helen Cowie · *Lobster* Richard J. Kin · *Monkey* Desmond Morris · *Moose* Kevin Jackson
Mosquito Richard Jones · *Moth* Matthew Gandy · *Mouse* Georgie Carroll · *Octopus* Richard Schweid
Ostrich Edgar Williams · *Otter* Daniel Allen · *Owl* Desmond Morris · *Oyster* Rebecca Stott
Parrot Paul Carter · *Peacock* Christine E. Jackson · *Pelican* Barbara Allen · *Penguin* Stephen Martin
Pig Brett Mizelle · *Pigeon* Barbara Allen · *Polar Bear* Margery Fee · *Rat* Jonathan Burt
Rhinoceros Kelly Enright · *Salmon* Peter Coates · *Sardine* Trevor Day · *Scorpion* Louise M. Pryke
Seal Victoria Dickenson · *Shark* Dean Crawford · *Sheep* Philip Armstrong · *Skunk* Alyce Miller
Snail Peter Williams · *Snake* Drake Stutesman · *Sparrow* Kim Todd · *Spider* Katarzyna and Sergiusz
Michalski · *Swallow* Angela Turner · *Swan* Peter Young · *Tiger* Susie Green · *Tortoise* Peter Young
Trout James Owen · *Vulture* Thom van Dooren · *Walrus* John Miller and Louise Miller
Wasp Richard Jones · *Whale* Joe Roman · *Wild Boar* Dorothy Yamamoto · *Wolf* Garry Marvin
Woodpecker Gerard Gorman · *Zebra* Christopher Plumb and Samuel Shaw

Polar Bear

Margery Fee

REAKTION BOOKS

To Lou, for coming to see the polar bears with me, and everything else

Published by
REAKTION BOOKS LTD
Unit 32, Waterside
44–48 Wharf Road
London N1 7UX, UK
www.reaktionbooks.co.uk

First published 2019
Copyright © Margery Fee 2019

Printed and bound in China

A catalogue record for this book is available from the British Library

ISBN 978 1 78914 146 7

Contents

Introduction 7

1 Early Encounters 23

2 It's a Bear's Life 45

3 Arctic Spectacle 79

4 Entertaining Polar Bears 103

5 It Takes Two to Tangle 137

6 Save the Polar Bears! 165

Timeline 184

References 186

Select Bibliography 210

Associations and Websites 212

Acknowledgements 215

Photo Acknowledgements 216

Index 219

Introduction

In a few generations we've turned into sclerosed
super-specialists, each in a niche so tight that our limbs
can't stretch and our brains can't turn.
Charles Foster, *Being a Beast*[1]

We've all seen a photo of a polar bear standing alone on an ice
floe: it symbolizes the warming climate and the disappearing bear.
It evokes reactions of sympathy, guilt, irritation, grief or anger,
sometimes more than one. These reactions are often labelled 'political', as if a human world without politics existed. Things get even
more complicated if you start thinking about the bear's perspective
or that of people who live closely with polar bears in the Arctic
or at the zoo. This particular bear, for example, is not lost or in
trouble on that floe, which is where it has evolved to be at home.
At least, it is not in trouble as long as it has a floe to stand on.

The photo cuts the bear off from any human context quite
thoroughly, as many nature photos do. Images of polar bears that
depict them in a radiant glow of timeless perfection in a trackless
snow-world – or the opposite, snarling, dying or dead – vastly out-
number those that show them going about their daily life in the
twenty-first century, stretched out on gravel, casing refuse dumps,
interacting with zoo visitors, eviscerating seals or swinging
unconscious in a net under a helicopter. It is our desires, our fears
and our politics that make animals into icons and cram them with
meaning.

Although polar bears were known to mid-eighteenth-century
natural historians, the way in which polar bears were connected
to the much more widely distributed brown bear was disputed for

Polar bear on
an ice floe in
Ukkusiksalik
National Park,
Nunavut, Canada.

7

a long time. The polar bear's official Latin name, *Ursus maritimus* (sea bear), was not completely fixed until 1971: for a while it was named *Thalarctos*, a combination of two Greek words, *thalasso*, 'sea', and *arctos*, 'bear'. Some scientists did not see the polar bear as belonging to the subfamily *Ursinae*, which includes all other bears except the giant panda (*Ailuropoda melanoleuca*) and the Andean bear (*Tremarctos ornatus*). Now it has been proved that polar bears evolved from brown bears and still are quite closely related to them. As we will see, as they evolved, characteristics of brown bears were kept or discarded, depending on what supported survival in the extremely cold temperatures of the Arctic on a diet consisting almost exclusively of seals.

Polar bears live on the interface between ice and water; for us, they live on the interface between nature and culture. Unlike many even more seriously endangered species, which include tigers, rhinos and orangutans, polar bears have always, like

Polar bear swim, Vancouver.

other large exotic animals and top predators, been a focus of
human imagination.[2] For Indigenous hunters, these bears carry
huge meaning, one that comes out of knowledge traditions quite
different from those of the dominant culture. However, these
hunters have been engaged in the international fur trade for
hundreds of years and resist stereotypes that would, for example,
restrict them to hunting solely for food using traditional methods.[3] Further disputes arise among those who promote an
expansionist commercial approach and those who would temper
this approach by considering Indigenous sovereignty, animal
rights or environmental protection.

The title of this book – *Polar Bear*, rather than *Polar Bears* –
indicates the aim of the Animal series to synthesize what is known
about particular species from a variety of cultural and disciplinary

Mother and
cubs, Ukkusiksalik
National Park,
Nunavut.

perspectives. This synthesis brings scientific generalizations based on large numbers of observations together with more imaginative representations, including those focused on the stories of individual animals. The latter approach, deemed sentimental by some, is reflected in nature artist Ernest Thompson Seton's title *Wild Animals I Have Known* (1898). At the extreme, one could say that art particularizes; science generalizes. Scientific accounts are not supposed to evoke emotion; like the photo of the bear on the ice floe, they may narrow the field of vision to an abstracted creature. Such accounts of animals avoid the personal or the emotional for fear of projecting human attributes onto their subject, a projection that is often criticized as anthropomorphism. But this criticism goes too far in reserving intelligence and feeling solely for us. For the medieval Norse, the polar bear had the wit of eleven men and the strength of twelve.[4] For the Inuit, the polar bear is exceptional in its intelligence, its *isuma*. Although some might scoff at these assessments, they are the conclusions of those who met the bear face to face on the ice over millennia. The reduction of 'true knowledge' to the statistical, the objective and the economic leaves out other perspectives, knowledge that might be useful in understanding the current situation of the polar bear and its melting homeland.

So let us consider not only the scientific consensus on polar bears, but the stories about them and the clashing and sometimes highly emotional disputes they generate. This approach allows for the idiosyncratic and the personal, including the stories of particular bears like Mad Bess, Alaska, Knut, Bärle, Binky, Gus and Linda, who moved into the human social world as individuals. Cultural history resists presenting empirical facts as all that matters; science resists the exclusion of reason and empirical testing. In 1802, as science became an ever more powerful institution, the Romantic poet and engraver William Blake argued that wisdom required a fourfold framework that combined the factual, the sensual, the emotional and the spiritual. He declared, 'May God us keep / From single vision & Newton's sleep!'[5] His engraving of Isaac Newton was his representation of the single vision of empiricist science, both its masculine power and its mechanical narrowness.

To weave all four of Blake's perspectives together is difficult. However, consider that at least since the signing of the Agreement on the Conservation of Polar Bears in 1973, we have learned a huge number of facts about them, extending to their genome and their gut microbiota. But these scientific facts do not explain why the sexiest actresses and movie stars have posed on polar bear rugs, why the most heroic men have been depicted fighting them hand to hand or why people often dress up as polar bears.

The mainstream representation of polar bears has changed over time. Once, heroic explorers confronted a snarling beast intent on killing them. Here is an example of the type of description that supports that image, published in 1831:

> This fierce tyrant of the cliffs and snows of the north unites the strength of the lion with the untameable fierceness of the hyena . . . he is sometimes left for weeks without food, and the fury of his hunger then becomes tremendous. At such periods, man, viewed by him always as his prey, is attacked with peculiar fierceness.[6]

Now, although this narrative of a vicious man-killer continues, it has been joined by a new story about the 'vanishing polar bear'. As Jon Mooallem writes, 'The first polar bear tourists started arriving in Churchill [Canada] thirty years ago to see a bloodthirsty

Imster Schemenlaufen carnival parade, Imst, Austria.

mankiller – an enigmatic Lord of the Arctic. Now we'd all come to see a delicate, drowning victim.'[7]

Although polar bears do not speak much except in Coca-Cola commercials, they have many spokespeople, not all of whom agree: Polar Bears International, the International Union for the Conservation of Nature Polar Bear Specialist Group (IUCN-PBSG), the World Association of Zoos and Aquariums, governments, hunters, animal rights activists and many others, even some who use polar bears to argue that we humans are not responsible for climate change. Polar bears have been called 'polarizing bears' for good reason.[8]

Writers from outside the Arctic quickly developed conventional ways of describing the region:

On the 19th of August [1773] we sailed from this uninhabited extremity of the world, where the inhospitable climate affords neither food nor shelter, and not a tree or shrub of any kind grows amongst its barren rocks, but all is one desolate and expanded waste of ice, which even the constant beams of the sun, for six months in the year, cannot penetrate or dissolve.[9]

Indeed, the tundra is empty and barren for most of the year, but the many hours of summer daylight produce an immense burst of life, mainly in the ocean, which then feeds a huge number of creatures, including humans, who manage to find food and shelter in this 'uninhabitable' place. The polar bear sits at the top of this web of life, its apex predator and the world's largest terrestrial carnivore.

The perspective of the Inuit and other Arctic Indigenous peoples on polar bears and the Arctic remains quite different from that of newcomers. For them, polar bears are respected and powerful beings and the Arctic is home. John Ross, a British explorer famous for his expeditions in search of the Northwest Passage, encountered Tulluachiu and his family in 1830 on the eastern coast of the Boothia Peninsula. Tulluachiu had lost his leg to a polar bear; the ship's carpenter made him a wooden leg, which allowed him to go hunting again. Ross commented of the Inuit he met that although they were a group 'so small and secluded, occupying so apparently hopeless a country, so barren, so wild, and so repulsive', they enjoyed 'so perfect vigour, the most well-fed health, and all else that here constitutes, not merely wealth but the opulence of luxury since they were as amply furnished with provisions, as with every other thing that could be necessary to their wants'.[10] Explorers, on the other hand, were cold in their woollen clothing and ill from inadequate food. The Indigenous peoples of the Arctic produced ethical and intellectual ways of being that supported not just their survival, but a rich culture that nonetheless was generally classified by (shivering, starving) outsiders as primitive. Indigenous beliefs and attitudes are recorded in early rock and cave art, small bone and ivory carvings and oral stories, all produced long before Arctic peoples met those from the south. And many of these beliefs and attitudes persist.

For people who would never go there during the Age of Discovery, the Arctic worked as a vibrant imaginative space. It was a remote world populated by mysterious peoples and creatures, lit by famous atmospheric effects such as the Aurora Borealis and the Novaya Zemlya effect. These images provided a halo of romance and heroism even to expeditions undertaken mainly for commercial and imperial gain. What we know about polar bears between the settlement of Greenland by the Norse and the First World War comes mainly from the accounts of explorers and whalers, although missionaries and fur traders also played a part. As the Age of Exploration moved on to the Age of

J. Brandard, lithograph from an original sketch by John Ross, 1830. Left to right: Shulanina, Tulluachiu, Tirikshiu.

Revolution and then to the Industrial Revolution, polar bears moved from being a rare gift reserved for monarchs to starring in an array of enterprises in natural history, science, exploration, commerce and education. Once central to tales of male heroism and imperial rivalry, they moved into an ecological discourse as a species in need of protection. Field scientists replaced explorers or hunters in images of polar bears.

North Pacific Ocean

ALEUTIAN ISLANDS

Bering Sea

KURIL ISLANDS

occupied by the Soviet Union in 1945; administered by Russia; claimed by Japan

JAPAN

Sea of Japan

Petropavlovsk-Kamchatskiy

Sea of Okhotsk

Khabarovsk

Kodiak

Bethel

Gulf of Alaska

Bristol Bay

Providesniya

Anadyr'

Magadan

Okhotsk

CHINA

Anchorage

Nome

Bering Strait

Arctic Circle

Oymyakon

Yakutsk

Valdez

UNITED STATES

Chukchi Sea

Pevek

Cherskiy

Juneau

Whitehorse

Fairbanks

Verkhoyansk

120

Prince George

Dawson

Prudhoe Bay

Barrow

Wrangel Island

East Siberian Sea

Tiksi

Fort Nelson

Inuvik

Beaufort Sea

sea ice extent summer average 2000-2006

NEW SIBERIAN ISLANDS

Fort McMurray

Yellowknife

Banks Island

Laptev Sea

Cambridge Bay

Victoria Island

Arctic Ocean

SEVERNAYA ZEMLYA

RUSSIA

CANADA

QUEEN ELIZABETH ISLANDS

Churchill

Arviat

Gjoa Haven

Resolute

Noril'sk

Yenisey

Rankin Inlet

Repulse Bay

Ellesmere Island

Kara Sea

Dikson

Hudson Bay

Pond Inlet

Alert

FRANZ JOSEF LAND

Iqaluit

Baffin Island

Baffin Bay

Qaanaaq (Thule)

Nord

NOVAYA ZEMLYA

Kuujjuaq

Davis Strait

Greenland (DENMARK)

Longyearbyen

Svalbard (NORWAY)

Barents Sea

Yekaterinburg

Perm'

60

Labrador Sea

Sisimiut (Holsteinsborg)

Ilulissat (Jakobshavn)

Bjørnøya (NORWAY)

Murmansk

Arkhangel'sk

Nuuk (Godthåb)

Ittoqqortoormiit (Scoresbysund)

Greenland Sea

White Sea

Severnaya Dvina

Kazan'

Samara

Qaqortoq (Julianehåb)

Tasiilaq

Jan Mayen (NORWAY)

Lake Onega

Nizhniy Novgorod

KAZ.

Denmark Strait

Norwegian Sea

Lake Ladoga

Saratov

Reykjavik

ICELAND

Arctic Circle

NORWAY

FINLAND

Helsinki

Saint Petersburg

Moscow

North Atlantic Ocean

Faroe Islands (DENMARK)

SWEDEN

Tallinn

EST.

Voronezh

Volgograd

Tórshavn

SHETLAND ISLANDS

Oslo

Stockholm

Baltic Sea

Riga

LATVIA

LITH.

Vilnius

Minsk

BELARUS

Kharkiv

Rostov

Krasnodar

Copenhagen

Kaliningrad

RUS.

Dublin

IRE.

Belfast

U.K.

Amsterdam

NETH.

DENMARK

Berlin

Warsaw

POLAND

Kyiv

UKRAINE

Sochi

London

Brussels

BEL.

GERMANY

Prague

CZECH REP.

SLO.

Chişinău

MOL.

Black Sea

North Sea

ROMANIA

TURKEY

Scale 1:39,000,000

Lambert Azimuthal Equal-Area Projection

0   500 Kilometers
0   500 Miles
     30

For a long time, for most people, polar bears were a only rumour because their habitat is so remote from major population centres. Further, as top predators polar bears are few, and in their habits mainly solitary. Not many people see polar bears even in the Arctic: they rarely go very far inland and prefer the ice. The biggest city inside the Arctic Circle is Russia's Murmansk (population around 300,000). However, communities where polar bears are routinely encountered are far smaller. In Alaska, Kaktovik (population 260) and Utqiagvik (formerly Barrow, population 4,200) are important to polar bears, who forage on the remains left there by Indigenous whaling.[11] The total human population of the Norwegian Svalbard archipelago, an important polar bear habitat, is 2,700. And Churchill, Manitoba (population 900), where polar bears do stroll the streets, is well below the Arctic Circle, at the same latitude as mainland Scotland's northernmost point. Only 4 million people live inside the Arctic Circle, of which approximately 500,000 are Indigenous. They are the Aleut, Gwich'in and Athabaskan peoples from North America, the circumpolar Inuit peoples, the Sami people from northern Scandinavia, and the forty 'small-numbered' peoples represented by the Russian Association of Indigenous Peoples of the North.[12] And of course, the estimated 26,000 polar bears.

The Arctic is defined variously by latitude (66°33′ 47.0″), by climate (the line representing the mean summer temperature of 10 degrees C (50 degrees F), or by vegetation (the treeline, where the boreal forest stops and the tundra begins). The last two lines vary between around 58 and 70 degrees of latitude. The Arctic Circle marks the northernmost point at which the sun is visible during the northern winter solstice, around 21 December. During the summer solstice, around 21 June, this is the line where the

Map of the Arctic region, 2012.

sun is still visible at midnight. In the High Arctic, the sun sets in October and doesn't rise again until late February. Winter temperatures can plunge to minus 50 degrees c (minus 58 degrees f) and stay that way for days or weeks.

The treeline runs south of the Arctic Circle to include the shores of the Bering Sea between Alaska and Russia. In Canada it swoops south to include Hudson Bay. All of Greenland is included in this definition: it has no boreal forest. Google Maps has been to the Arctic: no polar bears show up, but you do get a sense of the landscape. Search for Quttinirpaaq National Park or Iqaluit or Churchill to have a look.

The circumpolar Arctic is not evenly inhabited by polar bears, for whom ice, not land, is most important. And, as with porridge and Goldilocks, they need ice that is not too thick and not too thin. Scientists have divided polar bear populations into nineteen subpopulations, although some polar bears roam far and wide. These subpopulations are not very genetically diverse, but they are affected by different human regimes and other circumstances, including exposure to pollution, radiation, military installations, oil rigs and shipping.

The Arctic was named after the ancient Greek word for bear, *arktos*, because its lands are found under the constellation Ursa Major, Latin for 'great bear'. In many languages, the name for polar bear translates literally into English as 'white bear' or 'ice bear'. In Russian, it is *beliy medved*; in French, *ours blanc*; in Norwegian and Danish, *isbjørn*; in Icelandic, *ísbjörn*. It has also been called 'swimming bear'. The full scientific name of the polar bear is *Ursus maritimus* Constantine Phipps, 1774, because of the convention of adding to the name of a species the name of the person who first provided a scientific description and the year they did so.

The circumpolar Indigenous peoples speak many languages and thus have many names for polar bears. The best known is from

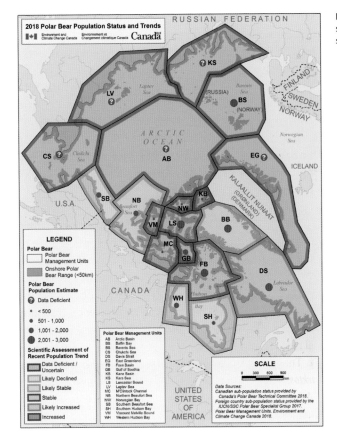

Polar bear subpopulation and status map, 2018.

Inuktitut: *nanuq* (*nanoq, nanook, nanok* and so on). The examples below come from the Inuit languages spoken mainly in Greenland and Canada, which are part of the wider Eskimo-Aleut language family. This language family also includes the Yupik languages spoken in parts of Alaska and in a few villages in Siberia. The Inuit often name the polar bear indirectly. To gossip about polar bears is to risk bad luck in the hunt. Nanuq is the king of the *iqsinaqtuit*,

Sidney Hall, *Ursa Major*, astronomical chart showing a bear forming the constellation, in Sidney Hall, *Urania's Mirror* (1825).

'those who make one frightened'. Similarly, the Sami in northern Scandinavia refer indirectly to the polar bear as 'the old man in the fur cloak' or 'God's dog'. The Ket, a Siberian people, call the polar bear *gyp*, 'grandfather', or *orqoi*, 'stepfather'. In eastern Greenland, the polar bear is called *tornassuk*, 'the master of the helping spirits'.[13]

One cliché about the Inuit is that they have a hundred words for snow, a generalization that might make them seem exotic or even obsessive. However, Inuktitut grammar forms one long word where English requires a sentence. And as specialists in polar bears, the Inuit have names for bears of different ages and in different situations. Apart from *nanuq*, in Igloolik, Nunavut, where these names were gathered, a newborn cub is known as *atiqtalaaq*; a young cub out of the den, *atiqtaq*, and a mother with cubs, *atiqtalik*. The cub that has just been booted into the world on its own is *avinnaajuk*, 'one separated from its mother'. Bears in dens are called *apitiliit*, 'those that have snow to cover them'. A fully grown male is called *angujjuaq*, 'must be feared'.[14] Further, *nanuq* in ordinary language becomes *pisukti*, 'the walker', in shaman's language and *pisuqasiaq*, 'the ever-wandering one', in poetic language.[15]

Other polar bear hunters have other names: the James Bay Cree call the polar bear *wâpûsk*; the Sayisi Dene (Chipewyan), *sas delgegiq*, *sas delgei*; Gwich'in, *chehzhii*; Aleut, *tanĝaaĝim*. Even polar bear scientists have specialist terms: *coy* means 'cub of the year'. Nineteenth-century European whalers called the polar bear 'the farmer' because of its ponderous, pigeon-toed walk.

Polar bears have been central to those who lived in the Arctic for millennia. However, as we will see, they entered the popular imagination in more southern regions as the quest for northern passages from Europe to Asia ramped up in the eighteenth century. Explorers' accounts, travel writing, natural histories and illustrated magazines and newspapers considered the polar bear the 'lord of the Arctic' and the Arctic itself as 'the last imaginary place'. Writers and artists depicted polar bears and the Arctic in works glorifying or questioning imperial ventures. Polar bears began to arrive in person and in public in southern zoos and circuses. However, during the twentieth century popular representations of polar bears began to shift. In 1973 the polar bear was singled out in the Agreement on the Conservation of Polar Bears because of concern about overhunting. Zoos and circuses were pressured to stop displaying animals that clearly did not do well in captivity. The former terrain of smiling 'Eskimos' and dauntless explorers became threatened territory as fears about global warming took hold. Two widely viewed documentaries, Al Gore's *An Inconvenient Truth* (2006) and the 'On Thin Ice' episode from the BBC television series *Frozen Planet* (2011), showed the polar bear amid scenes of melting ice. Greenpeace, the World Wide Fund for Nature, and other organizations took up the cause of protecting the polar bear and its habitat. Often, Indigenous concerns and opinions were overlooked in these more recent representations, just as they had been in the age of imperialism. Inuit writers, film-makers and artists are now working hard to explain why a ban on hunting leaves them economically and culturally at risk. Polar bear scientists have started to write popular books as well as scientific papers, hoping to convince the public that global warming is a real threat to polar bears – not without criticism from those who see climate change as a hoax. Polar bears, once seen as shadowy figures in a far-off place, have become the centre of controversies around Indigenous sovereignty, scientific credibility and climate change.

1 Early Encounters

After 600 years
the ivory thought
is still warm
Al Purdy, 'Lament for the Dorsets'[1]

Al Purdy's 'Lament for the Dorsets' was written for a vanished Arctic people whose carvings reveal a strong connection to polar bears. Their Inuit successors as well as the Norse who colonized Iceland, Greenland and small outposts in North America also regarded the polar bear with a respect marked in art and story. As large, rare and exotic animals, they were claimed by rulers as their royal perogative, who displayed them to enhance their power. Gradually, however, as more and more ships ventured out to find Arctic sea routes, polar bears were increasingly commodified.

Polar bears emerged as a species at least 400,000 years ago, according to recent genetic studies.[2] (*Homo sapiens* emerged in Africa around 300,000 years ago.[3]) But when did the two species first meet? One answer is provided by ancient carvings and pictographs.

If you try to sketch a polar bear, you will understand why it is not always clear whether the outlines carved by ancient peoples in caves or on rocks are actually intended to be polar bears. And written references to 'pale' or 'white' bears may not connect to polar bears either. Although polar bears are always white or yellowish white, confusingly, not all bears with light coats are polar bears.[4] Some subspecies of the black bear have pale coats, such as the rare Kermode or spirit bear (*Ursus americanus kermodei*) from the west coast of Canada. Brown bears (*Ursus arctos*) can also have pale coats, for example, the now critically endangered Himalayan brown bear (*Ursus arctos isabellinus*), which sports a coat described as 'sandy'. Hunter-naturalist James Lamont wrote in 1861, 'Individual bears of U. arctos are found frequently of a silvery grey colour, and such bears are known in Norway as "silver bears."'[5] The Ininkari bear is a brown bear with a white coat found in the southern Kurils, an archipelago that runs northeast from Hokkaido, Japan, to the tip of the Kamchatka peninsula. This colour phase is named after an Ainu chieftain, whose portrait shows him leading two cubs, one brown and one white.

Did early artists give their polar bears the arched Roman nose and the long neck that distinguishes them from brown bears, whose noses are more dished and shoulders more humped? Compared to brown bears, most polar bears seem positively streamlined. Most images of bears carved on rock faces or in caves are assumed to be brown bears (*Ursus arctos*) or cave bears (*Ursus spelaeus*). Cave bears went extinct around 24,000 years ago near the end of the Last Glacial Maximum. The bears depicted at Chauvet, France, dated around 30,000 years ago do have the dished noses of cave bears.[6] However, pictographs dated to 2,500 years ago found on the Siberian coast have been identified as polar bears.[7] Two other early sites might also contain polar bear images. One dated to around 14,000 years ago appears on a ceiling of the Ekain cave in northern Spain. Could these be polar bears?[8] They do have the requisite slender necks and heads.

In support of this identification, polar bears must have moved south during the Last Glacial Maximum, which reached its peak around 26,000 years ago. Then, thick ice covered half of Great Britain and much of northern Europe. The ice did not reach Spain, so polar bears might have found refuge there. Similarly, rock carvings in Alta, Norway, dating from around 8,000 years ago depict bears and their tracks – but what kind? All this potential for

Hakyô Kakizaki, *Ininkari, Ainu Chieftain of Akkeshi*, 1790, in the 'Ishuretsuzo' series.

confusion gives one an appreciation of the practice of giving bears scientific names and describing their differences as accurately as possible.

Vladimir V. Pitul'ko's archaeological work on the Yana River has revealed that people lived in the Siberian Arctic at least 30,000 years ago, but he has found no evidence that they hunted polar bears. However, in 1989, Pitul'ko discovered a Stone Age site on

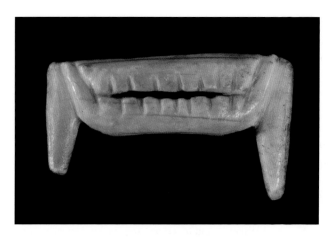

Zhokhov Island off the Siberian coast at 78 degrees north. Eight
thousand years ago it was inhabited by people who hunted reindeer and polar bears using dogsleds and stone, bone, mammoth
ivory and wooden tools.[9]

Debate continues about the earliest human settlement of
North America. The Bering Land Bridge from Asia to North
America was exposed between 20,000 and 10,000 years ago.
Genetic testing indicates that the peopling of the northernmost
part of the continent took place after an earlier wave of people
who went south along the coast. Around 5,500 years ago people
called pre-Inuit or Palaeo-Eskimo moved east across the North
American Arctic and Greenland. The Dorset people of the high
Arctic, the latest of these groups, flourished between 450 BC and
AD 1250. The Inuit call them Tuniit. Scholars have connected their
carvings of polar bears to shamanism or hunting magic, where
humans seek to be possessed by particular animals in order to
acquire special powers. As the shaman drummed and danced,
carved 'shaman's teeth' were slipped into a human mouth to
enhance the transformation. Other small, striking carvings also

demonstrate familiarity with the poses bears typically take in real life. The 'flying bear', thought to represent a spirit journey, can also be connected to a typical stalking pose, where the bear flattens itself on the ice, or to a bear swimming.[10] Carvings of men and bears either attached to each other or designed to slot together clearly represent a special relationship. According to the most recent thinking, the Dorset/Tuniit were displaced by the Thule people, the ancestors of the contemporary Inuit. The Thule quickly moved west from northern Siberia across northern North America all the way to Greenland between AD 1000 and 1330. The most likely explanation for the disappearance of the Tuniit (invariably described as mysterious) was an inability to adapt to the Medieval Warm Period (c. AD 950 to c. 1250). However, the

Nicolas Maréchal, *Ursus Maritimus* (*The Polar Bear*), 1808, engraving by Simon-Charles Miger.

URSUS MARITIMUS   L'OURS POLAIRE. (Serious de la Grandeur.)

Dédié au Citoyen Faujas - St-fond, Professeur de Géologie au Muséum National d'histoire Naturelle, Inspecteur des Mines de France &c. par le Citoyen Miger.

Middle Dorset flying bear carving, AD 500–1200, walrus ivory, Igloolik, Canada.

Inuit tell stories of taking over Tuniit lands, remembering them as 'strong people, but timid and easily put to flight and it is seldom heard that they killed others'.[11] Whatever happened, the Tuniit respect for polar bears continued in succeeding Arctic Indigenous cultures.

For the Indigenous people who hunted polar bears, the bears were valued as much as spiritual guides as for their meat, fat, sinews and warm fur. Indeed these values were interconnected, since all animals were seen as giving themselves only to the hunter who respected them and who followed the appropriate protocols after their death. However, for the Norse and the Russian Pomor settlers, live polar bears were far more valuable than dead ones if presented to European monarchs. The use of exotic animals as symbols of royal prestige and the popularity of staged bloody fights between animals meant that polar bears turn up in Europe and even further south more often than one might expect. Indeed, polar bears are said to have fought in ancient Rome: 'The Roman poet Calpurnius Siculus . . . described a day at the circus, in which not only were the crowds delighted with the beasts of the forest, but they also watched with enthusiasm the combat between the bears of the sea (presumably polar bears imported from the north) and the local "sea-calves."'[12] In 270 BC a celebratory procession staged by King Ptolemy II of Egypt was reported by his contemporary, the Greek writer Athenaeus, to have included a white bear.

In the second half of the tenth century (the beginning of the Medieval Warm Period), the Norse began to move west to Iceland, Greenland and northern North America. They raised cattle and carried out a trade in pelts, eiderdown, seal and whale blubber, walrus ivory, narwhal horns and the occasional live polar bear. The trade was based mainly out of the port of Bergen in southwest Norway.

The Norse did not take the power of the polar bear lightly. Like the Inuit, they referred to it obliquely, although perhaps as much for poetic reasons as out of fear or respect: 'the seal's dread', 'the

Dorset man-bear carving.

rider of icebergs', 'the sailor of the floe' and 'the whale's bane' are descriptive epithets found in early Norse literature. And Norse warriors known as 'berserkers' or 'bear-shirts' engaged in practices that resemble the shamanic transformations of the Inuit. In the thirteenth century Snorri Sturluson wrote of these men:

Ó□inn could bring it about that in battle his opponents were struck with blindness or deafness or panic, and their weapons would cut no better than sticks, while his men went without mail and were as wild as dogs or wolves,

Helmet plate patrix depicting a dancing warrior and a bear warrior (Old Norse *berserkr* or *úlfheðinn*), Öland, Sweden.

30

biting their shields, being as strong as bears or bulls. They killed the people, but neither fire nor iron took effect on them. That is called berserk fury.[13]

The bears in question might not have been polar bears. But one image of a berserker biting his shield comes from a chess set – the Lewis chessmen – dating to the late twelfth century. It is made of whales' teeth and walrus ivory, the latter certainly sourced in polar bear country.

Obtaining polar bear skins, not to mention capturing live bears, was arduous work. Some polar bears helpfully drifted on ice floes from Greenland to the coast of Iceland. Only Grímsey Island, off Iceland's north coast, lies within the Arctic Circle. Nonetheless, there have been six hundred sightings of polar bears in Iceland since it was settled in the 800s (and certainly more sightings have gone unreported); the bears may even swim part of the way. At their closest Iceland and Greenland are only around 300 kilometres (190 mi.) apart and polar bears have been known to swim much further.[14] To this day polar bears continue to turn up: there have been five since 2001.[15] Because they pose a risk to people and the Icelanders' shaggy cattle and other livestock, they usually receive a lethal welcome. When a mother is killed, the tamer cubs are more easily captured. Polar bears sometimes became pets, the proof being early thirteenth-century laws that stated, 'If a man has a tame white bear, then he is to handle it in the same way as a dog and similarly pay for any damage it does.'[16] Icelanders whose pets threatened the neighbours' livestock, dogs or even the neighbours themselves might have considered either killing them for their valuable pelts or sending them to the king in hope of royal favour.

In around 880 Ingimundr the Old of Iceland gave two cubs to King Harald the Fairhaired of Norway and in return received an

The Greenland
coat of arms.

ocean-going vessel filled with timber, even then scarce in Iceland.[17] Gifts of polar bears could help to convince the king to allow one to set up a bishopric, profitable both spiritually and materially. Polar bear skins were welcomed as offerings to churches: in his 1555 travel guide *Description of the Northern Peoples*, Olaus Magnus described hunters donating white bearskins to the high altar of the Trondheim cathedral in Norway, 'so that during a period of dreadful cold the celebrant priest should not suffer frozen feet'.[18] By the thirteenth and fourteenth centuries almost every church owned a polar bear rug.[19] Imagine just how cold those winter services must have been.

One widely adapted rags-to-riches story about a polar bear is found in an Icelandic manuscript dating from around 1275, although the story is no doubt older. Auðun was, it was said, a poor Icelander who managed to travel to Greenland, where he spent everything he had on a polar bear. He took it all the way to Denmark and gave it to the king. The reward was the usual: a ship filled with valuable goods. For Icelanders, whose island provided little in the way of natural resources, the story highlighted the possibilities of Greenlandic trade. It also showed deference to family, monarchy and religion, as in between delivering the bear and returning home to look after his elderly mother, Auðun made a pilgrimage to Rome.[20] Certainly Greenland and polar bears were firmly linked in the European imagination by the fifteenth century: a polar bear still features on the Greenland coat of arms.

Whether Auðun's story is fact or fiction, monarchs displayed polar bears as prestige possessions and gave them as gifts. King Haakon IV of Norway reigned for 45 years, during which time he added Iceland and Greenland to his empire. He gave Henry III of England a polar bear, which arrived in 1252. The City of London was responsible for the bear; we know about it mainly because the king wrote letters about the support of the bear and its keeper.

It was housed in the Tower of London as part of a menagerie that usually included lions, the symbol of the monarchy, and other exotic beasts. King Henry wrote: 'Greetings: we command you that for the keeper of our white bear, recently arrived from Norway . . . ye cause to be had one muzzle and one iron chain to hold that bear without the water, one long strong cord to hold the same bear fishing or washing himself in the river Thames.'[21] Polar bears in the wild rarely catch the cod that swim in the deep Arctic waters, but have been spotted availing themselves of a salmon run. Trader George Cartwright mentioned seeing 32 white bears in one day feeding on salmon on the southern Labrador coast in the 1770s.[22] And on a very good day, the king's polar bear might have caught a seal in the Thames.[23]

Kendra Haste, *Polar Bear*, 2010–11, steel and galvanized wire sculpture, Tower of London.

Although ordinary Londoners were not admitted to the Tower, they would have had the thrill of seeing the bear on its excursions to the river. Another white bear arrived in 1287.[24] A contemporary of Haakon and Henry, the Holy Roman Emperor Frederick II is said to have given a polar bear and a white peacock to the sultan of Egypt, Malik al-Kamil Muhammad, in 1232. The bear was reported as swimming (presumably with its own 'long strong cord') in the River Barada, which runs through Damascus.[25] Around the same time, in the account of his travels to China published in 1300, Marco Polo speaks of white bears. His description matches that of polar bears, the largest of the bears: 'In the northern districts are found bears of a white colour and a prodigious size, being for the most part about twenty spans in length.'[26] He

Polar bear mosaiculture, Jacques Cartier Park, Gatineau, Quebec, Canada.

made no mention of any trade in these bears, but the use of rare and exotic animals in international relations continues, for example, in China's 'panda diplomacy'.

The permanent Norse colonies on the coast of Greenland are estimated to have reached a peak population of around 2,500, but the settlers had vanished by 1540.[27] The last known record was of a marriage celebrated in 1408, although archaeological studies show that Christian burials continued after this.[28] As with the Dorsets, archaeologists are still arguing about why the Norse settlements vanished. Most explanations include the impact of a cooling climate at the end of the Medieval Warm Period.

The Russian Pomor settlers established themselves around the White Sea, a large inlet of the Barents Sea that contains the port of Arkhangelsk. Despite being icebound for five months of the year, it was Russia's chief seaport between 1584 and 1703. The English Muscovy Trading Company, founded in 1555, used this port until around 1700. The Pomors hunted for reindeer, Arctic fox, seal, walrus and polar bears from Svalbard to Novaya Zemlya, an archipelago off the Siberian coast. They may have captured the polar bears that arrived at the Swedish court in 1626 and 1685, the latter a gift from the tsar of Russia. Like the bears belonging to Henry III and the sultan of Egypt, they were allowed to swim in a nearby river, in this case the Strömmen, and to fish for their dinner.[29] Their royal owners spent much more on the bears than on their keepers. As literary historian Barbara Ravelhofer puts it: 'Exalted by their masters, these beasts reached beyond the animal world into the human domain of favor and privilege. They metamorphosed into hybrid courtiers.'[30] David Klöcker Ehrenstrahl's painting of a royal polar bear is as much portrait as natural history painting.

As far as we know, the Inuit had Greenland pretty much to themselves from the 1500s until a Christian mission succeeded in getting a toehold there in 1721.[31] Even in the absence of regular contact, Greenland was remembered:

> In the sixteenth century, as the royal power became more and more absolute, the king decreed that any pelts of such animals as foxes and polar bears, the teeth of walrus, etc. acquired in Iceland, must be offered for sale to the royal officials and only with their permission to others. This ordinance [dated 20 March 1563] remained in effect for centuries.[32]

Christian IV, king of Denmark and Norway, sent out several expeditions to Greenland in the early 1600s. Although they were generally unsuccessful, the polar bear became a national symbol.

Once European nations began to compete to find a northern commercial route between Europe and Asia, descriptions of polar bears appeared often in a variety of documents. Getting from Europe to Asia before the completion of the Suez Canal in 1869 and the Panama Canal in 1914 required long, dangerous voyages around the Cape of Good Hope near the southern tip of Africa (a route discovered in 1488) or Cape Horn, the southern tip of South America (discovered in 1616). It seemed logical that the Arctic might provide shorter northern routes, which it would have, except for the ice. Because it was known that the sun shone for 24 hours at the North Pole at summer solstice, a mistaken but persistent notion developed that the sea around the pole was clear of ice in summer.

Columbus thought he had reached India when he arrived in the Caribbean in 1492, which explains why he named the people he found there Indians. Many explorers credited with discovering Canada were, in fact, looking for the Northwest Passage. John Cabot was the first, dispatched by Henry VII in 1497. Jacques

One of the two
polar bears
on the roof of
Copenhagen City
Hall, Denmark.

Cartier, commissioned by Francis I of France, sailed up the Saint
Lawrence in 1535. The rapids where he stopped are still called
'Lachine', a reminder that China once was thought to lie just
beyond. His ship encountered polar bears near Funk Island off
the northeast coast of Newfoundland: 'Notwithstanding that
the island lies fourteen leagues from shore, bears swim out to it
from the mainland in order to feed on . . . birds; and our men
found one as big as a calf and as white as a swan that sprang into
the sea in front of them.'[33] Some say Funk Island was named for
the stench of guano from nesting sea birds, including the great
auk. European cod fishermen had killed all the great auks there
by 1800, and by 1844 they were extinct everywhere. The day after
spotting this swimming bear, Cartier's crew killed and ate another,
deeming it 'as good as a two-year-old heifer'.[34] Martin Frobisher,
an Elizabethan privateer, made three expeditions to Baffin Island
between 1576 and 1578. On one of them, a polar bear 'served them
for good meat for many days'.[35]

Despite immense effort, huge financial investment and many
deaths, the Northwest Passage was not crossed by sea until 1906.
Roald Amundsen and a crew of six took three years to get the *Gjøa*,
a shallow-draft boat, through the ice. During this trip, Amundsen
learned survival skills from the Netsilik Inuit, including how to
manage a dog team. These skills allowed him to reach the South
Pole in 1911 a month before his rival, Robert Scott. On one trip,
he acquired a pet polar bear. Despite Amundsen's achievement,
the Northwest Passage remains impassable for commercial use,
although likely not for long.

The Northeast Passage is said to have been traversed during a
very warm year, 1660, by a Portuguese explorer, but the first con-
firmed traversal was made in 1878. The Dutch explorer Willem
Barentsz set out to discover this passage in 1594, and tried twice
more, in 1595 and again in 1596. What we know about Barentsz's
voyages comes primarily from the diary of one of his officers,

Gerrit de Veer, which was quickly translated from Dutch into many languages. This rather boring account of sightings and soundings suddenly comes alive with the entry of a polar bear, and the publisher made the best of it with detailed and attractive engravings.

Barentsz and his men encountered their first polar bear in July 1594 on an island in the Svalbard archipelago. The crew killed it, as it did not take well to being captured.[36] They also discovered an empty bear's den on the ice.[37] On the next voyage the following year, two sailors were killed by a polar bear while absorbed in looking for 'stones, which are a kind of diament'.[38] On a third voyage in 1596, the expedition arrived at Spitsbergen, the largest island in the Svalbard archipelago. Sailing east, Barentsz's crew of sixteen men and a boy became trapped for the winter on

Barentsz's men and a polar bear, in Johannes Isacius Pontanus, *History of Amsterdam* (1611).

Novaya Zemlya. They built a house ('The Saved House') out of driftwood and ship's timbers. They were constantly harassed by bears as they moved supplies from the ship. Although they killed bears, they rarely ate them, relying on their ship's stores and foxes they trapped.[39] They did use the polar bear fat for lighting and kept the skins.[40] However, when they were finally preparing to leave, presumably running short of food, they ate polar bear.

> Her death did us more hurt then her life, for after we ript her belly we drest her liver and eate it, which in the taste liked us well, but it made us all sicke, specially three that were exceeding sicke, and we verily thought that we should have lost them, for all their skins came off from the foote to the head.[41]

This is the first documentation of the effects of an overdose of vitamin A, which polar bears accumulate in their liver, and which is toxic to humans. Like pork, bear meat can harbour *Trichinella*, a parasitic worm that can be killed by thorough cooking. Trichinosis has been advanced as an explanation for the deaths of many explorers, often already weakened by scurvy caused by the lack of vitamin C in their diet of ship's biscuit, salt meat, oatmeal, cheese, beer and spirits. Opinions on the taste of polar bear meat vary, which may depend on how fat the bear or how hungry the explorer. For example, in 1619, the Danish explorer Jens Munk (also Munck) and a crew of 63 became ice-bound near present-day Churchill, Manitoba. Munk reports:

> In the morning early, a large white bear came down to the water near the ship, which stood and ate some Beluga flesh, off a fish so named which I had caught the day before. I shot the bear, and the men all desired the flesh for food,

which I also allowed. I ordered the cook to just boil it slightly, and then to keep it in vinegar for a night, and I myself had two or three pieces of this bear-flesh roasted for the cabin. It was of good taste and did not disagree with us.[42]

The 'slightly boiled' meat may have contributed to the deaths of all the men except for Munk and two others. These three recovered from scurvy in the spring and, amazingly, managed to sail back to Denmark. One of the problems faced by many expeditions was the lack of wood in the tundra to cook food: the Inuit often eat raw meat and blubber (a prime source of vitamin C), but avoid polar bear liver and, unlike most explorers, know the signs of parasite-infested meat.

While Constantine Phipps was drafting the first accepted scientific description of the polar bear on his 1773 voyage, members of his crew were interacting with the bears in more direct ways. The youngest was fourteen-year-old Horatio Nelson, who, the story goes, sneaked off to kill a polar bear. When his rifle misfired he resorted to trying to club the bear with it. He was saved when the ship's gun was fired, scaring the bear away. Interrogated, he said he had wanted to give the skin to his father. This account, like the rags-to-riches story of the pious and dutiful Au☐un, is almost too good to be true. Historian Huw Lewis-Jones notes that no mention is made of it in the records of the expedition, nor did Nelson himself mention it. The first version appears in 1800, said to be based on the memory of an officer on the expedition. After Nelson died in 1805 after securing the British victory over the French navy at Trafalgar, this story circulated widely. It was just the thing to inspire high-spirited young boys to participate in dangerous imperial enterprises. Accompanied by a wide variety of illustrations, it has been repeated and embellished ever since,

Nelson's Adventure with a Bear, 17[...]

Postcard, 1905, from a painting by Richard Westall, *Nelson and the Bear*, 1806.

a recent version appearing in a comic strip published in 2003.[43] Polar bears were worthy adversaries for heroic British men, also busy killing tigers in India and lions in Africa as they learned to rule the waves and the rest of the world.

Another now-famous member of Phipps's crew was the formerly enslaved Gustavus Vassa, employed by the ship's naturalist and doctor. During his lifetime he used the name given to him by one of his owners. He is remembered today as Equiano because of the success of his life story, published as *The Interesting Narrative of the Life of Olaudah Equiano* (1789) during the campaign to abolish the slave trade. Equiano learned his trade as a young boy working for his owners in the Royal Navy and later as a merchant in the Caribbean, where he eventually earned enough to buy his freedom. Of the voyage with Phipps he commented: 'We killed many different animals at this time, and, among the rest, nine bears. Though they had nothing in their paunches but water yet they were all very fat. We used to decoy them to the ship sometimes by burning feathers or skins. I thought them coarse eating, but some of the ship's company relished them very much.'[44] Nonetheless, Equiano welcomed the fat, as it provided light for his quarters. Equiano was one of four African able-bodied seamen on the expedition.[45] These men were likely among the first from Africa to see (and eat) polar bears.

Daniel Orme
after W. Denton,
*Olaudah Equiano,
or Gustavus Vassa.*

Although they ate polar bears and took their pelts when they could, explorers were focused mainly on finding and mapping sea routes and producing scientific knowledge. The whalers who followed them had a more direct commercial goal: supplying the demand for whale oil and the fat from other Arctic mammals to light Europe's burgeoning cities.[46] Steam-powered whalers, rocket-propelled and explosive-bearing harpoons and breech-loading long-range rifles developed during the nineteenth century made whaling more productive and whales, walruses, seals and polar bears more vulnerable. Polar bears were at first taken as a sideline, but as whale numbers declined, whalers began hunting bears as a commodity. The polar bear was transformed from a spiritual guide, a monarch's prize and a highly respected foe into a commodity.

2 It's a Bear's Life

Here's the scientist, here's the Inuvialuit. If you put
them together, things would work better, with our
knowledge of what we know up here, and the scientist
with his knowledge, maybe they could come up
with something.
John Lucas, Sachs Harbour, *NWT*[1]

Detailed knowledge about polar bears for those outside the north
had to wait until the Age of Exploration. Ships, often carrying
artists and naturalists, returned with plants, animals and even
people from the territories they visited. Published accounts of
voyages were more than exciting reading. They were scoured, not
only by those looking for profitable sea routes, but by naturalists
seeking to fill their vast encyclopaedias with the latest accurate
information. Missionaries kept climate and natural history records,
as did the Hudson's Bay Company factors who became expert
naturalists, corresponding with Linnaeus and other naturalists
about Arctic wildlife.[2] In the early period, language differences
and colonial attitudes meant that Indigenous knowledge was dis-
counted, although the most successful explorers adopted Inuit
clothing, dogsleds and other technologies. What counts as scientific knowledge in the dominant society has lately come to include
what is called Traditional Ecological Knowledge (TEK), produced
by Indigenous peoples, or Inuit Qaujimajatuqangit (IQ). The
expression Local Ecological Knowledge (LEK) is also used for the
knowledge developed by those working closely within a given
ecosystem for utilitarian ends. Field scientists certainly develop
LEK and learn about TEK, but ultimately they aim at testing theor-
etical models or hypotheses by discovering empirical evidence.
They often generalize beyond the local and are expected by the

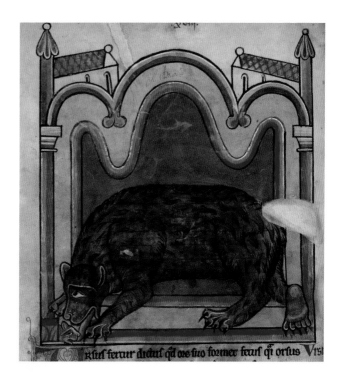

Bear licking
a cub into shape,
from a bestiary
of 1230–40.

research institutions who pay them to publish their findings in the context of peer review and feedback. Although there can be considerable agreement among these forms of knowledge, their different goals and contexts may generate misunderstandings. The Inuit have long lived with and thought about polar bears in ways that scientists do not. Now, Inuit politicians, activists and hunters are pointing out that their millennia of accumulated wisdom should be respected in policy and ecological debates.

Scientific writing based on careful observation of live animals or dead specimens began in classical times, although it was often mixed with speculation. The *Natural History* of Pliny the

Elder (first century AD) reported that newborn cubs are a 'lump of white unformed flesh, little bigger than Rats, without eyes and without hair; only the Claws are put forth. This lump, by licking, [the mothers] fashion little by little.'[3] Given that cubs are born blind, nearly hairless and weighing only 500 g–1 kg (1–2 lb) – tiny relative to their adult size – Pliny's account can be traced to observation. And because of his influence, we still lick people into shape (metaphorically).

Jacques de Sève, 'The Polar Bear', in George-Louis Leclerc, Comte de Buffon, *Collection of Quadruped Animals* (1754).

Enlightenment naturalists like the Comte de Buffon and Carl Linnaeus (both born in 1707) were undecided about whether the polar bear was a distinct species. Linnaeus listed the polar bear under the brown bear as *Ursus maritimus albus-major, articus* in his *Systema naturae* (1758).[4] Certainly the relationship between polar bears and brown bears has since been proven to be close. The polar bear in Buffon's colossal Enlightenment encyclopaedia *Natural History* (1749–1804) looks like a depressed weasel. But the artist does get its major prey right: the illustration by Jacques de Sève shows the bear with a half-eaten seal. And to be fair, this polar bear does have the narrow head and long neck of a polar bear. In his book Buffon also included a white 'land bear' that supposedly wandered in the forest, perhaps because he thought

John Webber, 'A White Bear', engraving by Peter Mazell, from James Cook, *A Voyage to the Pacific Ocean* (1784).

48

that Hudson Bay was too far south to provide a good home for an ice bear. Buffon's thin and hungry-looking polar bear influenced other artists, but natural history illustrators soon recorded the fat phase of polar bear life.[5] (Polar bears can double their weight when the seal hunting is good.) On his third and last voyage in 1778, James Cook was stopped by a wall of ice at about 70 degrees of latitude as he tried to move through the Bering Strait. The artist on this voyage, John Webber, produced a happy, even hippoesque polar bear. Buffon also gave a good explanation for the separation of the polar bear from its brown bear relatives: 'Isn't it likely that if we took one of our Savoy bears to the mountains of Spitzberg, if it found nothing to eat on land it would plunge into the water to search for food?'[6] (The last Savoy bear was killed in 1893, alas.)

Early European settlers, usually missionaries or fur traders, often kept systematic records of climate, local peoples, and flora and fauna. The Moravian missionaries who moved to polar bear territory – Greenland in the early 1700s and the Labrador coast in the 1770s – were also keen natural historians who recorded their polar bear encounters and even sent two specimens to Germany.[7] James Isham, the Hudson's Bay Company factor at Fort Churchill, noted of the year 1747, 'More [polar] Bears about this fort this fall than ever was knowne.'[8] He was the first to record that female polar bears denned in the area. The fur trader Samuel Hearne reported seeing black bears swimming for hours, catching insects in the water near Churchill:

> This was in the month of June, long before any fruit was ripe, for the want of which [the bears] fed entirely on water insects, which in some lakes we crossed this day were in astounding multitudes. The method by which the bears catch those insects is by swimming with their mouths open, in the same manner as the whales do.[9]

Charles Darwin's evolutionary tree describing the relationships among groups of organisms, 1837.

Based on this report, in the first edition of *On the Origin of Species*, (1859), Charles Darwin mused that

> Even in so extreme a case like this, if the supply of insects were constant, and if better adapted competitors did not already exist in the country, I can see no difficulty in a race of bears being rendered, by natural selection, more and more aquatic in their structure and habits, with larger and larger mouths, till a creature was produced as monstrous as a whale.[10]

Darwin's detractors ridiculed this passage, suggesting that he thought bears could transform themselves into whales, and he removed it from subsequent editions. However, he found an ally in James Lamont, a Scottish nobleman who made hunting expeditions to Svalbard in 1858 and 1859. Lamont supported Darwin's ideas about how a bear might evolve based on a particular stable food supply: 'I have stated that I conceive the Polar bear to have become a Polar bear by living on seals.' He continued, 'It is therefore to be supposed that the seal and the walrus were originated first.'[11] Lamont's account fits with the facts as now known:

> It surely requires no very great stretch of imagination to suppose that this variety was originally created, not as we see him now, but by individuals of Ursus arctos in Siberia, who finding their means of subsistence running short, and pressed by hunger, ventured on the ice and caught some seals . . . Then it stands to reason that those individuals who might have happened to be palest in colour would have the best chance of succeeding in surprising seals, and those who had most external fat would have the best chance of withstanding the cold. The process of natural

selection would do the rest, and Ursus arctos would, in the course of a few thousands, or a few millions of years, be transformed into the variety at present known as Ursus maritimus.[12]

Lamont answered those who might wonder why brown bears no longer seem to be 'catching seals and turning white' by pointing out that to do so they would have to out-compete the polar bears, who were better adapted to seal hunting. The same argument works in reverse: those who think polar bears will successfully turn to terrestrial prey in the face of ice loss don't take into account that grizzly bears are better adapted to the ecological niche of the tundra and fiercely defend their territory. Darwin responded warmly to Lamont's ideas and credited him with the independent discovery of the principles of evolution.[13]

Although Lamont's story gives a fair idea of how polar bears evolved from brown bears, questions remain about when this happened. The scientific consensus is that polar bears are the most recently evolved of the bear species, and that bears evolved from the Canidae (wolves, dogs, foxes and so on). The bear's other close relatives are the Pinnipeds (seals, walrus and so on), and the Mustelidae (weasels, raccoons, skunks, red pandas and so on). The first species deemed to be ancestral to the bear line is *Ursavus elmensis*, a creature the size of a fox terrier that lived 27 million years ago.[14]

The consensus among mammalogists is that there are eight modern species of bear in the family Ursidae in three subfamilies. The giant panda (*Ailuropoda melanoleuca*) is the only member of the subfamily Ailuropodinae. The spectacled bear, also known as the Andean short-faced bear (*Tremarctos ornatus*), is the only member of the subfamily Tremarctinae. Paddington, hero of the children's books by Michael Bond, is an Andean bear.

The third subfamily, Ursinae, includes the rest: the North American black bear (*Ursus americanus*); the brown bear (*Ursus arctos*); the polar bear (*Ursus maritimus*), the Asiatic black bear (*Ursus thibetanus*); the sloth bear (*Melursus ursinus*) and the sun bear (*Helarctos malayanus*).[15] The polar bear has no subspecies. The brown bears in North America are classified as *Ursus arctos*, a species that ranges worldwide. In North America, it is popularly known as the grizzly, although scientists usually call it the North American brown bear. Some make a distinction between the grizzly and the 'big browns' that fatten up on the coastal salmon runs, for example, the Kodiak bear (*Ursus arctos middendorffi*) from islands off southwest Alaska. Except for the black bear and the brown bear, listed as of 'least concern' by the IUCN Red List of Endangered Species, all the other species of bear are listed as 'vulnerable'. However, some subspecies or subpopulations of the black and brown bear are endangered or critically endangered.

Bear family tree.

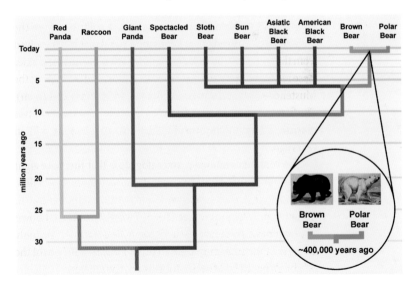

HEAD of a WHITE BEAR.

Andrew M. Skene, 'Head of a White Bear', in John Ross, *A Voyage of Discovery* (1819).

The giant panda was moved from 'endangered' to 'vulnerable' on that list in 2016 when its population still numbered less than 2,000. Given that the polar bear population is estimated to be around 26,000, why is it also listed as vulnerable? Its major prey is ice-dependent seals, who are threatened by climate warming. Further, it cannot be reintroduced into the wild from captive breeding programmes because polar bear cubs require at least two years to learn seal-hunting from their mothers to survive. Bamboo-eating pandas are better off: zoo-bred bears have been successfully reintroduced into the wild, although their habitat is also threatened by climate change and development.[16]

Until recently, the evidence for evolutionary history was fossils, bones and teeth, the latter not only because their hardness increases their chances of survival, but because they provide rough evidence of diet and age. However, few polar bear remains exist, presumably because most end up in the Arctic seas. The most complete ancient polar bear skeleton emerged from under the floor of a modern house in Norway in 1976; it is now on display in Bergen.[17] Ancient polar bear remains all date from the Pleistocene and often were found outside their current territory, presumably because glaciation forced them south.[18]

Genetic studies, however, are leading to breakthroughs in the knowledge of evolution and speciation. The first draft of the human genome was published in 2001 and completed in 2003. The polar bear genome was first published in 2010. In a 2014 article based on 79 polar bear genomes, which were compared to those of ten brown bears, the authors concluded that 'the species diverged only 479–343 thousand years BP [before the present]'.[19] An earlier DNA study of a polar bear jawbone found in Svalbard in 2004 concluded that polar bears had completely adapted to a maritime diet at 150,000 years BP.[20] New studies and discoveries are likely to revise these findings.

In fact, Darwin's famous evolutionary tree diagram, however useful, is not good at representing the hybridization that occurs during the process of speciation (what scientists call 'gene flow' and what we might call spur-of-the-moment sex). This hybridization complicates any story of a group of brown bears adapting during a particular cold period to become polar bears once and for all. The territorial ranges of polar bears and brown bears overlap, producing a fuzzy species boundary. Polar bears and brown bears have continued to interbreed: 'We find strong evidence of continuous gene flow from polar bears into North American brown bears after the species diverged.'[21] Presumably this interbreeding occurs more often during periods of Arctic warming. Recent discoveries of hybrid grizzly/polar bears in the Arctic by hunters have been traced to the preferences of one polar bear female, who has since died.[22] It is not clear that her preference

Hybrid bear, Osnabrück Zoo, Germany.

had anything to do with climate change. Zoos have also produced polar bear/brown bear crosses that have proven to be fertile in both females and males. However, hybrids may not fare so well in an Arctic hunting environment because their darker coat colour would reveal them to their prey.[23]

Although much more remains to be discovered about polar bear evolution, we know a great deal about their physiology and habits. The 1973 Agreement on the Conservation of Polar Bears committed its signatories to find out enough about polar bears to conserve them and their environment. What follows is a summary of knowledge gained mostly since the 1970s.

Like sumo wrestlers, polar bears must pack on the pounds. On average, full-grown females weigh 150–290 kg (330–650 lb) and are 2 m (6.5 ft) tall; fully grown males can weigh from 350 to more than 600 kg (775–more than 1,300 lb) and stand 2.6 m (8.5 ft) tall. Males are around twice as big as females. Because females do not mate while they are raising cubs, the annual male–female ratio is approximately one female to two or so males, which means lots of competition to mate. Older, bigger male polar bears dominate younger and skinnier bears, thereby getting more chances to reproduce.

Polar bears are the largest bear species and the largest terrestrial carnivore, although the Kodiak bear rivals them for size. Their size helps them withstand cold, since larger animals expose less of their surface area compared to their body mass. Fat is both

A male polar bear weighs between 350 and 600 kg.

insulation and energy store. Their ears and tails, smaller than those of brown bears, also conserve heat. Female polar bears must gain weight to sustain pregnancy and lactation; when pregnant they may go without food for eight months. For those tasked with observing how well polar bears are doing, there is a Polar Bear Scorecard to assess fatness with a scale from skinny to very fat. To allow for speedy weight gain, polar bears have stomachs that can hold 10–20 per cent of their weight and extremely efficient digestion (they use 84 per cent of the protein and 97 per cent of the fat).[24] They usually gobble their food: although humans are their only predators, their meal is at risk from bigger bears. They have the huge canines typical of carnivores and small molars compared to their omnivorous bear relatives, who eat a far more varied

Polar bear fatness index, illustrated by Emily S. Damstra.

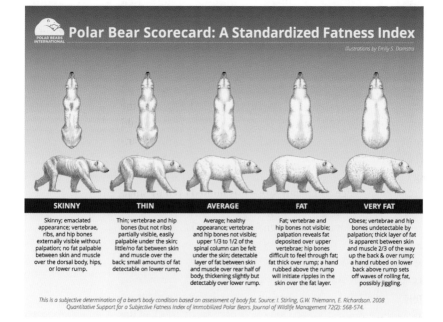

Polar Bear Scorecard: A Standardized Fatness Index

Illustrations by Emily S. Damstra

SKINNY	THIN	AVERAGE	FAT	VERY FAT
Skinny; emaciated appearance; vertebrae, ribs, and hip bones externally visible without palpation; no fat palpable between skin and muscle over the dorsal body, hips, or lower rump.	Thin; vertebrae and hip bones (but not ribs) partially visible, easily palpable under the skin; little/no fat between skin and muscle over the back; small amounts of fat detectable on lower rump.	Average; healthy appearance; vertebrae and hip bones not visible; upper 1/3 to 1/2 of the spinal column can be felt under the skin; detectable layer of fat between skin and muscle over rear half of body, thickening slightly but detectably over lower rump.	Fat; vertebrae and hip bones not visible; palpation reveals fat deposited over upper vertebrae; hip bones difficult to feel through fat; fat thick over rump; a hand rubbed above the rump will initiate ripples in the skin over the fat layer.	Obese; vertebrae and hip bones undetectable by palpation; thick layer of fat is apparent between skin and muscle 2/3 of the way up the back & over rump; a hand rubbed on lower back above rump sets off waves of rolling fat, possibly jiggling.

This is a subjective determination of a bear's body condition based on assessment of body fat. Source: I. Stirling, G.W. Thiemann, E. Richardson. 2008 Quantitative Support for a Subjective Fatness Index of Immobilized Polar Bears. Journal of Wildlife Management 72(2): 568-574.

Curio Joe, Proprietor Ye Olde Curiosity Shop Seattle

diet. Their ability to gain weight quickly is driven by the seasonal accessibility of their favourite food – seals. Polar bears eat around two-thirds of their annual intake between April and June, when the seals are pupping and moulting on the ice. (Think what it would be like if your refrigerator opened for only a few months a year.) The smallest Arctic species, the ringed seal, weighing around 50 kg (110 lb), is most polar bears' favourite food because of its circumpolar range and handy size – it is hunted even by small bears. Polar bears eat other things too, as we shall see.

Polar bears – apart from pregnant females – do not enter the deep winter hibernation typical of brown and black bears. Polar bears have to be active when seals whelp, mate and moult on the ice. In the early summer a polar bear's body weight can be as much as half fat. Then, with seals taking to the water and the ice retreating, most bears face a long fast. They spend much of the

J. E. Stanley, Ye Olde Curiosity Shop owner, posing with a polar bear rug, Seattle, postcard, 1913.

59

time dozing in little beds they make for themselves in snow or gravel. Fasting polar bears have been said to enter a state called 'walking hibernation' that enables them to better endure their long fast.[25] However, a study that from 2008 to 2010 tracked 24 polar bears fitted with temperature loggers in the Beaufort Sea on land, ice and water concluded that polar bears' metabolism while fasting did not change much more than that of any other fasting mammal.[26] Polar bears appear to balance low food intake with low energy output. Despite these constraints, polar bears can range widely while hunting, between 125,000 and 600,000 square kilometres.[27]

Compared to those of other bears, polar bear claws are short, broad and curved: good for grabbing fat, slippery seals and digging into the dens where ringed seals have their pups. Ringed seals have developed countermeasures, however. Other ice-dependent seals pup on the open ice, but the ringed seal's den protects the tiny new pups from polar bears, as well as from ivory gulls and foxes. As the bear digs through the roof, the seal and her pup have a brief moment to escape through their breathing hole. A six-week-old ringed seal pup can weigh a hefty 22 kg (48 lb). Pups are less wary than adult seals; polar bears take about a quarter of them in the den.[28] Sometimes the seals must dejectedly wonder if their main purpose is to turn the food they collect from the ocean into polar bear fat.

Bears hunt on the edges of landfast ice and at open areas called leads and polynyas (Russian, 'areas of open water surrounded by ice'). Except for landfast ice, polar ice is in constant motion, driven by wind and currents.[29] Leads are cracks caused by this movement or by tide action near shore. Polynyas are caused by winds, currents or upwelling warmer water and some, like the North Water Polynya (in West Greenlandic, *Pikialasorsuaq*, 'the great upwelling'), are semi-permanent. As the watering hole is to

the lion, so the breathing holes, leads and polynyas are to the polar bear. Polar bears are good swimmers, but not fast enough to reliably catch seals in the water. The ice is the bears' hunting platform, and they 'still hunt' (waiting motionless at the ice edge or beside a breathing hole until a seal pops up) or stalk their prey on the ice or from the water. They prefer to hunt on the edge of the annual ice over the coastal shelf, which is the most biologically productive region. Here the spring and summer sun nourishes algae on the underside of the ice, which in turn feeds the tiny creatures that feed the fish and larger animals. Thick multi-year ice is not good polar bear-hunting territory because it blocks the sun, and thus little life is found there. Nor can seals maintain breathing holes where the ice is thick. In the summer, when the annual ice melts, the bears retreat to multi-year ice or to land.

Polar bear 'still hunting', Franz Josef Land.

Mother seals leave their offspring to their own devices much earlier than polar bear mothers, whose cubs stay with them for two to three years; ringed seals are weaned by two months. Despite their inferior education and gormless expression, seals are no slouches at evading polar bears. One amazing video shows a bear engaged in a long complex stalk, first on the ice, then flattening for a splashless entry into the water so as to swim under the floe on which the seal is lolling. *Wham*, the bear emerges from the water in a ferocious lunge, but *whoops*, off goes the seal, leaving the bear standing wet and hungry on the now-empty floe.[30]

Despite the bear's fearsome reputation, this result is common. Even in good hunting areas, it takes a bear three to five days to catch a seal.[31] An adult polar bear needs to consume the fat from around 43 ringed seals or the equivalent to make it through the

John James Audubon, 'Polar Bear', in *The Quadrupeds of North America*, vol. II (1851).

Polar Bear

fast.[32] Bearded seals are much bigger than ringed seals, around 365 kg (800 lb); big male polar bears can flip them out of their breathing holes, a feat smaller bears can only dream of.

Charles S. Raleigh, *Law of the Wild*, 1881, oil on canvas.

Although seals are central in polar bear diets, if belugas or narwhals get trapped in the ice and are forced to surface for air in small holes the Inuit call *sassats*, bears have been known to surround and attack them. Groups of bears congregate to feed on beached whales, where they follow a social hierarchy topped by big adult males. Indeed, hungry bears will try anything: carrion, beavers, small rodents, waterfowl, shellfish, fish, eggs,

grasses, kelp, mushrooms, berries and – as with all bear species – rubbish.[33] However, the idea that they could compensate for a lack of seals by moving to a more terrestrial diet has been tested and found wanting. Although polar bears on land are generally described as 'fasting', they forage if they can. But if this foraging does not compensate for the days they lose on the ice hunting seals, it will not stop their populations from declining.[34] In Alaska, remains from Indigenous whaling have proved to be attractive foraging sites.[35] Although stranded whales are also a food source, and indeed might have contributed to polar bear survival in past interglacial periods when seals were in decline, the whale population has been much reduced.[36]

Polar bears can run at up to 50 kph (31 mph) for short distances, but overheat quickly. They prefer an easy strolling pace, unsuitable for chasing prey very far. A recent study that tracked seven adult females in the springs of 2014 and 2015 suggests that as ice conditions require them to walk or swim more to find seals, their condition will suffer and affect their reproduction rate.[37] These polar bears were tracked by small cameras on their necks. The camera angles are all over the place, but you do get to see the underside of a big blue tongue, the curious noses of other polar bears, and the frozen skinned seal that they are carrying around.[38]

Occasionally, polar bears will hunt adult walrus, the choice of very hungry bears, as the two big beasts are evenly matched. In 1990, Russian scientist Nikita Ovsyanikov arrived on Russia's Wrangel Island to conduct research. He was able to observe a beach packed with walruses and polar bears waiting for the ice to form. The bears' main tactic seemed to be to stampede the walruses in the hope that a vulnerable young one would be injured or left behind. Sometimes, they would harass an individual adult over days until it became too weak to withstand attack. Walrus skin is extremely thick (it was once marketed to make shoe soles and industrial belts); even polar bear canines are unable to penetrate it easily. Once a walrus is killed, several polar bears collaborate to pull it apart so as to be able to feed.[39]

Kaktovik food fight, Alaska.

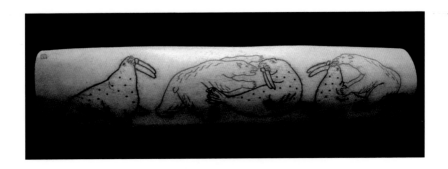

Hunting walrus, Chukchi carving, c. 1940, Regional Museum, Magadan, Russia.

Polar bears have an amazingly acute sense of smell: 'they may detect seal breathing holes up to 3 km away.'[40] The bears also use this sense of small to track female mates in the case of male polar bears or, in the case of polar bear mothers, to avoid males who pose a danger to their cubs.

Polar bears are highly motivated to learn, as their hunting skills make clear. The Inuit say that the bears have *isuma*, intelligence, and taught them to hunt.[41] They share tactics, including still hunting, hiding (humans behind a portable blind made of fox fur or white cloth, polar bears behind pieces of ice) and luring the mother to return to rescue her pup.[42] George Qulaut, Inuit hunter and member of the Nunavut legislature, describes just how clever polar bear tactics can be:

> It may scratch partway through the ice dome of the aglu [seal den], cover the opening with its body, and then settle down to wait until the seal arrives in the hole. Then it plunges its head through the thinned ice roof, and grabs the seal. By leaving the roof partially intact and blocking the light, the bear prevents the seal from becoming alarmed at the light streaming into its aglu . . . Once the bear has caught the seal, often by pinning it to the ice with its claws

66

and biting it, it pulls its prey up through the hole in the ice and snow. Although they may lack weight and strength, young bears rapidly learn these techniques by watching their mothers.[43]

Bears will also locate a den from above by smell and the hollow sound of the thinner ice over it, and then either break through the roof or swim underwater to catch the seal from below.[44]

Hunter in polar bear trousers carrying a blind, Greenland, 1999.

A 2016 study tested carnivore mammals in zoos using a 'puzzle box' baited with food: bears, including polar bears, led the pack, getting the food 70 per cent of the time.[45] The study drew two conclusions: brain size relative to body mass does indeed matter (bigger is better), and animals like meerkats, once thought to need high 'social intelligence' to negotiate their complex communal life, are terrible at puzzles. Polar bears do indeed have *isuma*.

Mortality in cubs during their first year can be as high as 50 per cent.[46] However, once polar bears make it to adulthood, females have a lifespan of around thirty years and males around 25. Some polar bears in zoos have lived past forty.[47] Male polar bears reach sexual maturity between six and eight years old, but normally don't mate until two years later because of the heavy

A mother and her cubs, 2001.

competition. Female polar bears reach sexual maturity around five years, but must weigh at least 200 kg (450 lb) in order to bear and raise cubs. They keep adding weight until they are around fifteen. If they are not nursing cubs, they enter a prolonged period of sexual receptivity (oestrus) between late March and early June, although most mating occurs in April and early May. Males can scent a female in oestrus and track her over long distances.[48] Female polar bears do not ovulate until they have been in contact with a male for up to two weeks – they spend a week flirting and a week mating. This induced ovulation reflects the usual distance kept by adult bears. Ovulating is pointless if fertilization is not possible. Coupled with this induced ovulation is delayed implantation of the fertilized ovum. The egg does not mature unless the female weighs enough in the autumn. If she doesn't, the egg is absorbed, and she mates again the following year.

Like all male bears, polar bears have a baculum, a penis bone.[49] Some scientists speculate that the baculum may have evolved to fend off other eager males by allowing for prolonged connection. Humans, it is thought, evolved monogamy to solve the problem (although slip-ups have been known to occur). Thus, there is no human baculum. Chimpanzees have the smallest penis bone of all primates, perhaps because a female chimpanzee will mate with as many males as possible – a tactic that ensures that her offspring will be spared by males who think they might be the father. These are competing genetic strategies: the males want to ensure paternal success at the expense of other males; the females to preserve their offspring, whoever the father. Female polar bears are not always faithful to the first comer either: sometimes fraternal twins have different fathers.[50] A difference in size between males and females of a species (sexual dimorphism) is explained in polar bears by the fact that bigger males are more successful at fending off the competition. Older male bears show the marks of injuries from fights, including broken teeth and scars around their muzzles that show the underlying black skin.

Pregnant females move into a den and hibernate until the birth of two, sometimes one and, very rarely, three, cubs. (Polar bear females have four nipples; brown bears, who may have four cubs, have six.)[51] The cubs are usually born in December and weigh a little more than an adult rat, between 500 g and 1 kg (1–2 lb). Although this apparently premature birth seems risky given the Arctic cold (often below minus 50 degrees c/minus 58 degrees f), the dens are warm, even without a huge fat-burning mother inside. Ian Stirling describes the den as an 'external womb'.[52] The bear feeds her cubs on high-fat milk (around 36 per cent fat, like whipping cream) until they weigh around 10–15 kg (22–33 lb).[53] The percentage of fat in her milk decreases as the cubs grow.[54] She then acclimatizes the cubs to the outside world for a few days before taking them to the ice edge where, finally, she can begin to hunt. Over the next two to three years, the cubs will stay with her, nursing and learning seal-hunting protocols.

Polar bears den on land or on sea ice; most dens are found on leeward ridges where the wind piles up snow of the appropriate consistency. If there is an unseasonable warm period, dens collapse, killing the mother and her cubs, and the same thing can happen to ringed seals. Those bears that den on land often return to where they were born. In Western Hudson Bay dens are dug into peat or sand ridges. In most areas, bears den close to the sea ice, which means a shorter trip to the ice with new cubs. In Western Hudson Bay the bears move inland, sometimes as far as 100 km (60 mi.) from the coast, perhaps because the peat there provides good insulation from the cold.[55] And in fact, dens there provide insulation from the heat, too; males use them during the summer. However, as temperatures rise and the land dries out, fire may threaten these dens.

Over the period between entering her den in late autumn and emerging with her cubs, between four and eight months, the female polar bear will not eat, urinate or defecate, losing nearly half her body mass.[56] She does not suffer from the build-up of urea in her blood (the condition that some humans require dialysis for),[57] nor does she lose muscle or bone mass (the problem astronauts face in zero gravity). This ability is shared with other hibernating bears.

Polar bears have other useful physiological adaptations. Sumo wrestlers are subject to Type 2 diabetes, as susceptibility rises roughly in tandem with body weight. Polar bears, however, manage their high-fat diet and huge weight gains and losses without obvious problems. They are not only adapted to a diet of almost pure fat, but are able to use the fat to supply their need for water (called 'metabolic water'). Eating snow or meltwater drains much-needed heat. Camels use a similar trick, although their fat

Mother sleeping with two cubs.

Polar bear
swimming.

is consolidated in their hump so the rest of their body can cool off. Adult polar bears usually eat only the fat from a seal, probably because protein requires more water than fat does to digest. Their leftovers serve to feed a trail of followers: adolescent bears, Arctic and red foxes, ivory gulls and ravens.

Since the hairs that make up polar bear fur are hollow, it was proposed in the 1970s that they act like fibre-optic cables, transmitting heat to the bear. If this were the case, however, the bears would heat up in summer, when they already have trouble keeping cool. This 'fact' still circulates, although it was debunked in 1998.[58] However, the air trapped in the fur does help to conserve heat. Another mistaken 'fact' that sometimes circulates is that well-insulated polar bears are invisible to thermal-imaging cameras.[59] The hairs are not white, but translucent; in the summer, after the moult in the spring, the bear's black skin may show through.

Polar bears in zoos sometimes turn green when algae grows in the hollow hairs. The coat has dense underfur coupled with long, shiny guard hairs that repel water and ice: the Inuit use a little pad of polar bear fur to build up ice on their sledge runners so they will not stick in the snow.[60] Polar bear paws are fur-covered and the pads have small bumps and indentations that allow for a better grip. The paws are also big relative to their owner's size, distributing their weight like snowshoes.

Polar bears rarely hunt in the water, but they are extremely good swimmers. Their partially webbed front paws help them to manoeuvre. One radio-collared female was tracked on a 687-km (427-mi.) swim in 2008; she swam for nine days and then walked for a further 53 days. She lost almost a quarter of her body mass and her year-old cub did not survive this epic feat.[61] Cubs do survive swims of less than 50 km (30 mi.) or so. The smallest ride on their mother's back. That said, sea ice loss means that bears are being forced to swim more and for longer distances, which takes more energy than walking. Swimming bears have drowned in storms, with cubs at the greatest risk.[62] Despite their adaptation to the cold, they go to considerable lengths to avoid getting wet in cold weather.

A huge focus for field scientists has simply been to find out how many polar bears there really are, a complex and still unfinished task. The 1973 Agreement on the Conservation of Polar Bears required that the parties 'conduct national research programmes, particularly research relating to the conservation and management of the species'. Now every polar bear seems to have its own scientist, bureaucrat and activist. Polar bears are under almost as much surveillance as city dwellers in the south. The IUCN Polar Bear Specialist Group website gives the most reliable numbers for fifteen of the nineteen subpopulations. The population of the other four (Arctic Basin, East Greenland, Kara Sea, Laptev Sea) is unknown. A 2018 study of the Chukchi Sea subpopulation of polar bears shows a healthy population of just under 3,000, despite increasingly longer ice-free periods there. Unlike the neighbouring Beaufort Sea subpopulation, which is declining, the Chukchi Sea bears benefit from their location in a region with a large continental shelf that supports more sea life.[63] The estimated total population is 26,000.

Methods for counting bears have been refined over time. 'Mark-recapture' refers to a method to prevent double counting: bears are marked, either by an actual tattoo or, more recently, by DNA testing. In the first form, a bear is darted with a tranquillizer, usually from a helicopter. Then the bear is given a lip tattoo and an ear tag, and has various bits taken for further testing, such as fur, fat, blood and a small molar. Female and young bears are sometimes outfitted with a satellite radio collar; collars won't stay

Polar bear jumping, Svalbard, Norway.

Lt Eric Davis supporting a sedated polar bear's head after placing an identification tag in its ear, 1983.

on adult male polar bears because their necks are so thick. The collars are programmed or remotely controlled to drop off after a set period.[64] Small ear-tag transmitters and other such devices are now beginning to replace the larger collars.

After this, the bear is further marked with temporary green dye on its rump to warn hunters not to kill the sleepy bear (unfair, not to mention that the meat is full of drugs). Bears recover completely from this process, even those who have been repeatedly darted.[65] In Churchill, Manitoba, where polar bear field research was first established, this method has been combined with the capture of 'problem bears'. If a bear reappears with green dye on its rump, it is wearing the equivalent of an orange prisoner's outfit.

In one type of genetic mark-recapture, the bears are darted from helicopters, but not tranquillized. The dart with its sample of hair and skin falls out and is collected later. The DNA profile

Polar bear with radio collar, Svalbard, Norway.

identifies the individual bear and its gender. This method is easier, but collects less information. Another form of mark-recapture uses DNA taken from hair snagged near whalebone piles or even from footprints.

How does mark-recapture translate into a population number? If in the first year a hundred bears are captured and marked, and in the next year a hundred bears captured but only ten are found to be marked, one can assume that there are roughly 1,000 bears out there.[66] This method assumes a 'closed population' (no births, deaths, arrivals or departures). Nonetheless, regular mark-recapture studies have, until recently, provided the best population estimates, as well as information about ages (from the tooth), lifespan, reproduction and contaminant loads.

However, in many vast territories, bears are few and far between. Some counting in these regions has been done with low-flying helicopters, which is both expensive and dangerous. Recent methods use drones and commercially available images taken from space.[67]

Much of the detailed knowledge outlined above has come from scientists working with tranquillized bears; this technique of using 'flying syringes' to immobilize wild animals for relocation or study was widely adopted only in the 1960s. The shift from killing bears for research was important. Nonetheless, some Inuit see even tranquillizing bears as repellent because it shows disrespect for a powerful and intelligent peer. The government of Nunavut prohibits the practice because they believe that manhandling is disrespectful and makes the bears more violent. The study on the use of satellite images was done in Nunavut with government approval.

Since polar bear hunting was completely banned in the Soviet Union in 1956 and remains banned in the Russian Federation, officials saw no need to count bears. As a result, 'next to nothing is known in Russia', particularly about the polar bears in the Leptov and Kara subpopulations.[68] Much of Russian polar bear territory overlaps with military or oil-production sites and, thus, is deemed off-limits for foreign scientists. In 2016, however, Russian and American scientists began testing a counting method that uses aircraft equipped with both thermal and digital cameras.[69]

Although both scientists and bureaucrats have begun to think about how to incorporate TEK into their own perspectives and policies, ultimately, Euro-Western beliefs are grounded on a sharp human–animal distinction while Indigenous concepts of personhood include both human and other-than-human animals.[70] A worldview so different, even at times contrary, to that of mainstream science takes time to understand and evaluate. As the book progresses I will canvass Indigenous views on polar bears along with those of polar bear scientists, eco-activists and others.

3 Arctic Spectacle

Witness the white bear of the poles, and the white
shark of the tropics; what but their smooth flaky
whiteness makes them the transcendent horrors
that they are? That ghastly whiteness it is which
imparts such an abhorrent mildness, even more
loathesome than terrific, to the dumb gloating
of their aspect?
Herman Melville, *Moby-Dick* (1851)[1]

In the century between the Napoleonic Wars and the First World
War, the Arctic was increasingly mythologized: if your reaction
to Melville is to beg to differ, your opinion has likely been condi-
tioned by more recently constructed mythologies. The polar bear
became a 'transcendent horror' as part of the history of exploration when, after the victory over the French, the British navy
needed to redeploy idle ships and men. Just as space exploration
became a focus of international rivalry in the 1950s, as well as
fostering ideals of men with 'the right stuff', so it had gone with
the Arctic. 'Arctic spectacle' galvanized public attention and
engaged the imaginations of artists and writers.

During this period, images became more and more widely
available: the illustrated *Penny Magazine* (1835–45) set off a wave
of imitators across the u.s. and Europe; the *Illustrated London News*,
the first weekly to feature images, was founded in 1842, when early
photographs began to be used as source material for engravings.
By the end of the century, 'One did not need to be a connoisseur
with a shelf of folio volumes and a private collection of art – the
same images, the same information, and the same sense of a
secured "possession" of images and facts could be obtained by
persons of very modest means.'[2] Gradually a discourse about
the Arctic formed, one that usually supported the principles of

imperialism and industrial development. The general public avidly read about explorers, particularly stories of the 'quests' to conquer the frozen north, often depicted as an allegorical woman dressed in clinging drapery (to be wooed and won or taken and used, depending on one's perspective). An image from *Punch* (1875) representing the 'Queen of the Arctic' with her attendant polar bears includes this verse:

But still the white Witch-Maiden, that sits above the Pole,
   In the snow-bound silver silence whose cold quells aught but soul,
   Draws manly hearts with a strange desire to lift her icy veil:

Hans Lindenstaedt, poster for the German Arctic Expedition, 1913.

The bravest still have sought her, and still will seek,
whoever fail.[3]

This highly masculinist and eroticized discourse has been used
to justify wars and imperialism. It exhorts men to discover 'virgin'
territory and bring civilization to foreign peoples. As a result, the
people John Ross described in 1835 as self-sufficient, even wealthy,
were transformed into colonial subjects.

In Joseph Conrad's *Heart of Darkness*, published in 1899, the
stalwart, trustworthy and very British narrator Marlow begins his
tale this way:

> Now when I was a little chap I had a passion for maps. I
> would look for hours at South America, or Africa, or Aus-
> tralia, and lose myself in all the glories of exploration. At
> that time there were many blank spaces on the earth, and
> when I saw one that looked particularly inviting on a map
> (but they all look that way) I would put my finger on it and
> say, 'When I grow up I will go there.' The North Pole was
> one of these places, I remember. Well, I haven't been there
> yet, and shall not try now. The glamour's off.[4]

As with a virgin – or in the case of the *Punch* poem, a 'witch-maiden'
– once another man has won her she is no longer desirable: to be
first is to conquer. For example, Roald Amundsen, on hearing that
Robert Peary had reached the North Pole in 1909, immediately
turned south, beating Robert Scott to the South Pole by a month
in 1911. The glamour that surrounded the imperial enterprise
shrouded its less glorious side, including many lives lost unnec-
essarily through bad planning, weak leadership, inadequate
supplies and bad luck. The quest for a first with respect to the
North Pole continues (by balloon, by plane, by submarine, by

John Tenniel after
Joseph Swain,
'Waiting to be
Won, Queen of
the Arctic', *Punch*,
5 June 1875.

WAITING TO BE WON.

(ARCTIC EXPEDITION SAILED MAY 29, 1875.)

snowmobile, on skis, by dogsled, on foot, solo without resupply and so on).

Few women played a direct role in Arctic exploration until the late twentieth century. Discovery of the poles or the Arctic sea routes became like the finish line in the Olympic men's hundred-metre dash: a male competition that enhanced both personal and national glory. Ursula K. Le Guin's short story 'Sur' reflects on the gendered nature of exploration.[5] She imagines the discovery of the South Pole the year before Amundsen got there by a group of rich South American women. They keep their accomplishment secret because they would be disbelieved, or, if believed, would be disowned by their husbands. The story also points to the Western focus on the documentation and proof that any regulated competition requires: there have to be winners and losers, even if they are separated by tenths of a second. And documented 'firsts' suggest that nothing came before, although Arctic Indigenous men, women and children may well have been the earliest visitors to that abstract, featureless but extremely desirable location. Indeed, polar bears probably made it to the North Pole long before the best accredited human claimants: several have been documented a mere amble away.[6] Now, the decline in summer ice means that getting there is ever easier and the list of 'firsts' includes tourists on cruise ships.

Our continuing intense focus on who was first and who was most prominent obscures the truth that these expeditions were the result of slow, incremental, complex and collective knowledge and hard work. And, as with any human enterprise, sacrifice and bravery have been mingled with much less admirable behaviour. Although a diverse group which included black men and Inuit men and women explored the Arctic and tried for the pole in the early days of exploration, their contributions have generally been downplayed or overlooked until recently. Expeditions were named after their leaders, and their leaders were white men. (Knud Rasmussen is often heralded as the first European man to cross the Northwest Passage by dog team, although he was born in Greenland and his mother was part Greenlandic Inuit.) And polar bears, when they were not threatening the explorers or eating their supplies, gave themselves to be turned into food and clothing.

Robert Peary's claim to the North Pole was and is debated; his evidence was not subjected to serious scrutiny until the 1980s.[7] And few know that Peary's 'first man' on seven expeditions over 23 years, including the 1909 claim to the pole, was an African American, Matthew Henson, whose memoir *A Negro Explorer at the North Pole* was published in 1912. He records that expedition

Polar bears near the North Pole approaching the submarine USS *Honolulu*, 2003.

members wore 'reindeerskin and polar bearskin clothing . . .
made for [them] by the Esquimo woman, Ahlikahsingwah,
aboard the *Roosevelt*', the ship that took them north from Greenland in 1909.[8] On the ship were '22 Inuit men, 17 Inuit women,
10 children'; four of these men went to the pole with Peary and
Henson – Ootah, Egigingwah, Seegloo and Ooqueah. Frederick
Cook, who claimed he had stood at the pole before Peary got
there, also had Inuit companions: Etukishook and Ahwelah.[9] In
1909 the journalist Lincoln Steffens hailed the battle over Peary's
and Cook's competing claims: 'Whatever the truth is, the situation

is as wonderful as the Pole,' he wrote. 'And whatever they found there, those explorers, they have left there a story as great as a continent.'[10]

As a result of the obsession with the Arctic, polar bears haunted the frozen and forbidding landscapes that quickly became etched in the popular mind. One example is Samuel Taylor Coleridge's long poem *The Rime of the Ancient Mariner*, published in 1798. The mariner's wanton killing of the albatross led to death for his shipmates and a lifetime of expiation obsessively recounting his story. French artist Gustave Doré included polar bears in one of his thrilling and gloomy illustrations for the 1877 edition of the poem, although Coleridge made no mention of polar bears – the ship was steered towards the South Pole. Perhaps they were expected in any such scenes of ice and snow. It was as if the many men who died of starvation, exhaustion and cold on polar expeditions had all been devoured by a vast polar bear.

Critics reflected on whether such representations inspired or merely titillated the reader or viewer. Art critic John Ruskin saw Doré's work as reflecting 'the corruption of the times . . . in terms of physical and sexual repugnance, and morbidity'.[11]

In 1816 Mary Godwin began to write *Frankenstein* in a villa near Geneva in the company of her future husband Percy Shelley, Lord Byron and a few others. The novel begins with the story of Captain Robert Walton, a rebellious young man eager for glory. Walton believes (like several real experts of the time) that he will find a warm land and open water north of Archangel and become famous for his scientific discoveries. Arriving in St Petersburg, he writes that the cold 'fills me with delight'.[12] He dreams of discovering the magnetic pole, 'the wondrous power which attracts the needle', making astronomical observations, satisfying his 'ardent curiosity with the sight of a part of the world never before visited' and treading 'a land never before imprinted by the foot of man'. And

Gustave Doré, illustration for Samuel Taylor Coleridge, *The Rime of the Ancient Mariner* (1877).

of course, he hopes to achieve glory 'by discovering a passage near the pole to those countries, to reach which at present so many months are requisite'.[13] Mary Shelley animates a whole set of clichés, clearly conveying how well the polar myth captured the imaginations of many young men.

Readers might wonder how to take this passage: do we admire Walton or see him as naive, grandiose and deluded? As Dr

Frankenstein's fate makes clear, Shelley had mixed emotions about men ardent for glory (a group that included her beloved and irresponsible husband). Later, Walton's ship rescues Dr Frankenstein, who has been pursuing his Creature northwards. The crew becomes restive as the ice thickens around them. Frankenstein rallies them with a rousing speech, but after he dies the tone shifts. The Creature appears on board to brood over his creator's body and reflect on his own misery, then tells Walton he is going to the North Pole to make his funeral pyre. The ship turns south and the novel ends with this apocalyptic image of fire, death and ice. Shelley, like her mother, Mary Wollstonecraft, author of *The Vindication of the Rights of Women* (1792), put feminine feeling before masculine glory. Frankenstein dies raving against the Creature who has killed his wife, family members and friends, never considering for a second the folly of first creating and then spurning him.

Walton's fictional attitudes were prevalent in mainstream society. In 1818, the same year *Frankenstein* was published, John Ross, like Walton, turned back from his attempt to find the Northwest Passage. The press ridiculed him for his caution, encouraged behind the scenes by his second-in-command and rival, William Parry. John Barrow, second secretary of the British Admiralty from 1804 to 1845, wrote an anonymous review of Ross's account of the voyage. He suggests that a summer expedition was merely 'a voyage of pleasure' and that Ross should have stayed through the winter to fully meet the expectations of a true Arctic explorer.[14]

Ross was lampooned by George Cruikshank, the famous illustrator of the novels of Charles Dickens. His cartoon shows Ross returning in pompous triumph, leading a procession bearing gifts to the British Museum. A dead polar bear marked with the constellation of Ursa Major is carried on a stretcher by men who have

Landing the Treasures, or Results of the Polar Expedition.!!!

lost their noses, either to frostbite or from greeting too many Inuit. Ross's account of the voyage says that 'nose pulling' was the traditional Inuit greeting.[15] In the rear follows a figure intended to be the ship's translator, an Inuit man called John Sackheouse. His only garment is a sort of tutu made of polar bear fur. Under one arm he carries an artist's portfolio and in the opposite hand he bears a narwhal horn. One of the sailors at the right-hand edge of the cartoon asks what will happen to 'Jack Frost', meaning Sackheouse. The reply is 'Cut his throat and stuff him . . . I suppose', the likely fate of the 'Eskimaux dogs' in the procession.[16] One target of the cartoon was the British Museum and its scientists' desire to house and display dead animals and even dead people.[17] What was the point of such expensive expeditions, which brought nothing home of practical use? However, one of the plates contained in Ross's account was drawn by Sackheouse, which was 'certainly the earliest representational work by a Native American to be so reproduced'.[18]

William Parry got his chance to lead expeditions in 1819, 1824 and 1829, which, while finding neither the Passage nor the Pole, surpassed the exploits of previous explorers. In order to boost morale, he encouraged his men to produce an on-board newspaper,

George Cruikshank, *Landing the Treasures; or, Results of the Polar Expedition*, 1819, hand-coloured etching on paper.

which tellingly undercut the prevalent high-minded rhetoric of unmotivated heroism. The British Discovery of the Northwest Passage Act, passed in 1745, offered prizes for reaching particular stages on the route through the Northwest Passage, with £20,000 to whomever reached the Pacific. A shipboard poet produced this sally:

> Fired with fresh ardour, and with bold intent,
> Our minds shall, like our prows, be westward bent,
> Until Pacific's wave pour forth sweet sounds,
> Chiming to us like – Twenty thousand pounds![19]

As early as Martin Frobisher's 1576 expedition, which hauled tons of useless iron pyrite back to Britain because it was thought to be gold ore, wealth had featured in Arctic dreams. The Inuit taught their children never to show shiny rocks to white men, 'because it "steals their minds"'.[20] Although such expeditions aimed to discover something of commercial value, particularly the Northwest Passage itself, writers and artists also found their reports inspiring, at least if they agreed with Edmund Burke that the goal of the finest art was to be a 'source of the sublime':

> Whatever is fitted in any sort to excite the ideas of pain and danger, that is to say, whatever is in any sort terrible, or is conversant about terrible objects, or operates in a manner analogous to terror, is a source of the *sublime*; that is, it is productive of the strongest emotion which the mind is capable of feeling.[21]

One example of art aiming at the sublime is Caspar David Friedrich's *The Sea of Ice* (1823–4), also known as *The Wreck of Hope*; Parry's ship, HMS *Griper*, is barely visible, locked fast in the ice.

The Arctic was also featured at a popular venue in London's Leicester Square, the Rotunda, built in 1801 to house Henry Aston Barker's panoramas. These panoramas, like the popular engravings, allowed ordinary people to see images that once had been reserved for the elite. A round room with a circular painting of Arctic scenes placed visitors in the centre of a landscape, much as IMAX films do today. Romantic poets were among the early visitors, including John Keats and William Wordsworth.[22] Few Londoners could hope to see such scenes in real life; these precursors of films, television and the Internet gave them some idea about distant places.

John Franklin set sail to find the Northwest Passage on 19 May 1845, with a crew of 24 officers and 110 men, soon all to be lost. Strangely, Franklin's failure proved more inspiring of music, art and literature than many other men's successes in Britain, the U.S. and Canada, where he and his crew perished. Charles Dickens reported being 'filled with a sort of sacred joy' on reading accounts of such expeditions.[23] Charlotte Bronte's *Jane Eyre* was published in 1847, just as alarm had begun to circulate about Franklin's fate. The lonely orphan Jane amuses herself by looking at the Arctic landscapes in *Bewick's History of British Birds*, scenes that mirror her feelings. In Brontë's novel *Villette* (1853) the heroine's name is Lucy Snowe. The novel is filled with Arctic references: glaciers, Aurora Borealis and polar bears. As the heroines' names reveal, both novels play with the symbolic power of the elements. Ice serves as a metaphor for states of mind; descriptions of their mental difficulties show women characters demonstrating courage and resilience, qualities normally reserved for men like Franklin and his crew.

In 1864 Edwin Henry Landseer, famous for designing the four lions at the base of Nelson's column in Trafalgar Square, exhibited a painting at the Royal Academy inspired by the loss of the

Edwin Henry Landseer, *Man Proposes, God Disposes*, 1864, oil on canvas.

Franklin expedition. *Man Proposes, God Disposes* suggests that the prevailing enthusiasm for heroic discovery may be neither wise nor good. Like Doré's illustrations, the painting was praised for inspiring sublime terror and criticized for evoking revulsion and disgust. Landseer had based the painting closely on the factual description of the Irish explorer Francis Leopold McClintock, recounting the discovery of a ship's boat still containing remains of some of Franklin's crew. McClintock's book, *The Voyage of the 'Fox' in the Arctic Seas*, published in 1859, 'outsold works by Thackeray and Dickens' in the 1860s.[24] Darwin's *Origin of Species* was published the same year, with its implications of a material rather than a divine origin for life. Landseer may have been using polar bears as a stand-in for men. Reports of cannibalism among the crew had reached London, to be furiously repudiated by Lady Franklin and Charles Dickens as impossibly un-British.[25] The painting now hangs in Royal Holloway, London. Since the 1970s it has been covered when examinations are held in the same room, as rumours that anyone who sat near it went mad began to circulate. That Landseer had been confined to an insane asylum the year before his death in 1873 may have affected both the tone of the painting and the rumours.

Arthur Conan Doyle first came to public attention not with stories about a scientific detective but with stories, articles and lectures based on his youthful experience as ship's doctor on the whaler *Hope* in 1880. In his diary, he writes

everywhere are the bears. The floes in the neighbourhood of the sealing ground are all criss-crossed with their tracks, poor, harmless creatures, with the lurch and roll of a deep-sea mariner. It is for the sake of the seals that they come out over these hundreds of miles of ice – and they have a very ingenious method of catching them, for they will choose a big ice-field with just one blow-hole for seals in the middle of it. Here, the bear will squat, with its powerful

Caspar David Friedrich, *The Sea of Ice*, c. 1823–4, oil on canvas.

forearms crooked around the hole. Then, when the seal's head pops up, the great paws snap together, and Bruin has got its luncheon.[26]

He published 'The Captain of the Pole-Star' in 1883, a horror story told through the diary of the ship's doctor: unlike the captain of the *Hope*, this captain goes mad and walks off over the ice to his death. However, Doyle was also able to speak of the quest for the pole as 'a challenge to human daring' and describe the Arctic as 'a training school for all that was high and godlike in man'.[27] We might see contradiction, even hypocrisy in the distance between his diary's account of boredom, bloodshed and hard work on the ice fields and the open sea, his story of the madness of an Arctic whaling captain, and the soaring rhetoric of British imperialism. We might also consider to what extent that soaring rhetoric has been replaced by the discourses that see humans as saviours of the planet, rather than implicated, like the whalers, in its destruction.

W. G. Burn Murdoch, a Scottish artist and travel writer, was inspired by a boy's book, *Fast in the Ice* (1863) by R. M. Ballantyne. He was first engaged as an artist for a trip to Antarctica in 1892 that did a little light discovering while recouping its expenses with some serious sealing. Burn Murdoch's observations of polar bears on a 1913 expedition to Greenland are admirable and admiring:

A large fellow here was waiting for a seal at a hole in the ice, and a blue seal (Phoca Barbata) [a bearded seal] just showed itself, and apparently to take the chance, with one swoop of his forearm and claws, the bear threw the great six-hundred-pound seal well on to the ice and with a fore-foot on its back, broke the head off at one bite and drank the blood and wolfed up every bit of skin and blubber . . .

Of course it is an old bear which can do such a feat, possibly twenty years old and much bigger and broad in the quarter and shoulder than you can expect to find in Europe in confinement.[28]

Three polar bears traverse sea ice in southeast Greenland.

Finding few whales, the crew killed seals, and in one month, seventeen polar bears for the pelts.[29] Sometimes, they ate polar bear three times a day.[30] As with Au☐un, a live bear was a prize. The ship brought four polar bears – two adults, Port and Starboard, and two cubs, William and Cristabel – back to Europe. The bears spent their time caged on deck, loudly protesting their captivity and persistently dismantling their crates. The adult bears went to zoos (one in Spain, the other in Edinburgh) and the two cubs were sold 'for much moneys to a certain millionaire'.[31] Unloading the bears in Tromsø proved tricky:

Our bears' cages, all tattered wood and iron bars, were lifted, bears and all, by the winch over the side, and of course sank almost to water level. One of the iron bars was levered up a little with a crowbar, which gave, in Starboard's case, an opening for his delicate paw, which instantly came out and tore the cage to smithereens, and out he came, and evidently to his great content, wallowed about in the sea and washed his face, and took a dive or two and rubbed his paws, saying 'Bé-waugh' and 'B-e-a-r' frequently, and looked perfectly happy and amiable.[32]

It's hard not to like Burn Murdoch for his humour, self-deprecation and underdog Scottish nationalism. However, perhaps because he is writing for an audience of hopeful future whalers, he does not dwell on the idea that his expedition could find no 'commercial' whales because of over-hunting. Nor did he seem concerned about delivering four polar bears into captivity, although he did wonder, briefly, how the bear that went to Spain might do in the heat. The boyish and good-natured oblivion to personal danger inspired by British boys' books extended to nature itself – apparently nothing could harm it.

Not all narratives see polar bears as commodities, however. Stories about humans marrying bears are commonplace both in Indigenous and European cultures. Not surprisingly, polar bears enter the picture more rarely. A novella by James Hogg, known as 'the Ettrick Shepherd', 'The Surpassing Adventures of Allan Gordon' (1837), features a polar bear called Nancy. She becomes Bear Friday to the hero, Allan Gordon, who finds himself the sole survivor of a shipwreck near Greenland. Hogg veers between a realist account of how his hero survives from day to day and the horror he feels on surprising a polar bear plundering the wrecked ship's supplies. Gordon manages to kill the polar bear but discovers it has a cub, which he feeds on the whale blubber still stored in the wreck. Nancy is devoted; she hunts for him, even saving him from attack by a huge male bear, 'her first lover'.[33] They sleep in the same bed, and Nancy becomes more like a human bride, providing an analogue to 'selkie stories' where seal men and women transform into lovers for humans.[34] When Gordon manages to connect with some Greenlanders, he fears her jealousy and resolves to conduct his affairs with the young women when she is asleep. He marries only after Nancy has sunk into her winter sleep: 'What a strange life we led during the dreary and darksome winter months! We were actually little better than the bears lying in a torpid state.'[35] Once Nancy wakes up and finds she can no longer share his bed, she spends the nights groaning: 'I could not leave my wife and supposed beautiful inamoratta to sleep with a huge white she bear, and yet I had resolved to do it rather than drive her to desperation.'[36] Before he can make good on this plan, Nancy vanishes. The little community comes under attack by a group of polar bears that kill them all. One makes off with Gordon, taking him directly to Nancy. We wonder, will her jealousy prevail? That night, loyal as always, she secretly takes him to the coast. He finds a boat there and connects with a ship that takes him to Scotland. The story maintains the gulf between the inhabitants of the lands that British explorers felt the right to claim, while constructing a powerful bond between the hero and its most iconic predator. Many North American works of fiction suggest a similar transfer of power between animals symbolic of the land and their male heroes, for example William Faulkner's novella 'The Bear' (1942), or Robert Kroetsch's *The Studhorse Man* (1969). The loyal Nancy becomes symbolic of Greenland, like the Queen of the Arctic in the *Punch* cartoon, 'waiting to be won'. Both representations downplay or ignore the Indigenous inhabitants while inspiring newcomers to forge a sexual and spiritual bond with the land.

Folktales also describe intimate relationships between polar bears and humans, for example two Norwegian tales, 'White Bear King Valemon' and 'East of the Sun and West of the Moon'.[37] In 'White Bear King Valemon' a king's youngest daughter dreams of a golden wreath. The king orders his goldsmiths to make some, but none pleases her until she sees a white bear in the woods wearing the wreath that matches her dream. The bear says he will give it to her if she marries him and gives her three days to get ready. Shortly the plot begins to overlap with 'East of the Sun', where a girl also marries a bear who takes her to his castle. In both stories, the bear turns into a man when he comes to bed in the dark. Finally, curious to see him, each wife lights a candle. In both stories, the bear-man tells her that if she had managed to control her curiosity for a year, the spell condemning him to be a bear would have been broken. Now he will have to marry someone else. In both stories, the wife searches for him, using gifts from magical helpers. Eventually, each succeeds in finding her husband, he gets to remain a human prince, and you can guess the rest. However, in these stories, it is a curse to be a bear and a blessing to have a loyal wife.

In Inuit stories, polar bears enter a variety of relationships with humans: although they can turn into humans, they remain polar bears. Anthropologist Franz Boas, during research on Baffin Island, collected one about an old woman who adopts a polar bear cub. When the bear grows up, he hunts for her.[38] In this world, which does not see animals as distinct from humans in the same way as European stories, it is not a curse to be a polar bear.

The different perspectives on polar bears in Inuit and European stories is hardly surprising, not only because of broad differences in ways of seeing the world, but because in one

Kay Nielsen, illustration in Peter Christen Asbjørnsen, *East of the Sun, West of the Moon* (1922).

98

culture, polar bears were part of daily life and in the other rare and exotic creatures that came to symbolize a previously unknown part of the world. However, even in the British representations of the Arctic one finds differences of opinion on the value of Arctic exploration, from those who represented it as a heroic enterprise to those, like Mary Shelley and Landseer, who had their doubts. Nonetheless, by the end of the century, polar bears were firmly ensconced in Euro-American imaginations.

Theodor Kittelsen, *White Bear King Valemon*, postcard, 1912.

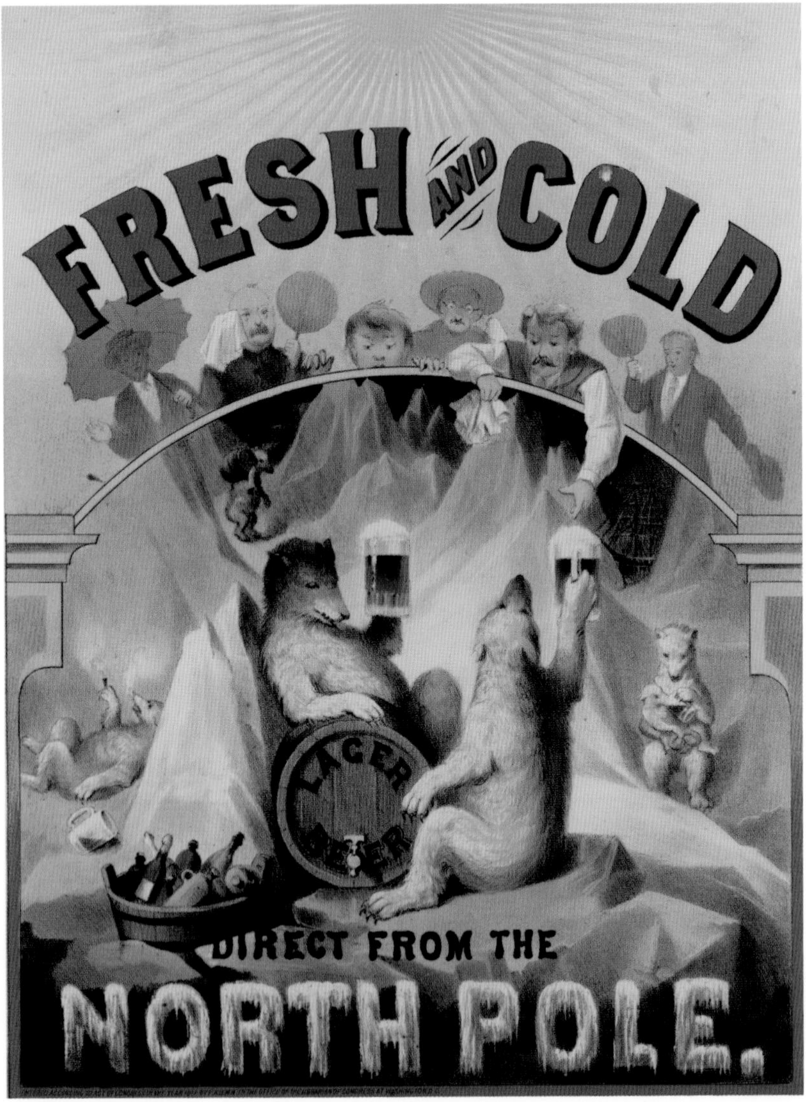
FRESH AND COLD
LAGER BEER
DIRECT FROM THE
NORTH POLE.

4 Entertaining Polar Bears

For heaven's sake, you can't be in love with a Polar Bear!
They hibernate. They moult. Their whole biology is different!
Geoff Ryman, *The Child Garden* (1989)[1]

Gradually, polar bears moved from the possession of kings and prelates to more public institutions: menageries and bear pits morphed into public zoos, private collections grew into museums and circuses became popular family entertainment. Formerly ferocious, polar bears are now cute, becoming toys for children and brand mascots for a variety of enterprises. At the same time, polar bears and their fur continue to be associated with luxury, wealth and power, including sexual power, as the practice of posing famous stars on polar bear rugs makes clear. Asserting this power nowadays are those who have made polar bears into one of the most highly regulated animals in the world: the bureaucrats and politicians who enforce the terms of the 1973 Agreement on the Conservation of Polar Bears and the scientists, some of whom hope to save the polar bear by storing their genetic material or with a variety of controlled breeding programmes, either in captivity or in the wild.

Before polar bears were well known in southern cities, their relatives were conscripted as entertainers at the highest level. Henry VIII built a bear pit at Whitehall; Elizabeth I organized bear-baiting contests for foreign guests. Bear-baiting pitted dogs against bear in something like televised wrestling matches – much of the choreography was designed to avoid fatal injury, at least for the bears. Bears were hard to replace. The Eurasian brown

Advertisement for 'Fresh and Cold Lager beer direct from the North Pole', lithograph by A. Hoen & Co., Baltimore, Maryland, 1877.

bear (*Ursus arctos arctos*) was extirpated in the British Isles before AD 1000; bears in London after that were involuntary immigrants. A waterman-turned-poet popular in the reign of James I, John Taylor, wrote that the bears were trained

> to dance, and (gravely grumbling)
> To fight & to be Active (bravely tumbling)
> To practise wards, and postures, to and fro,
> To guard himself, and to offend his foe.[2]

In fact, male polar bears mock-fight to prepare for the real fighting that determines their chance to mate. But baiting was far from mock for the bears and often deadly for the dogs.

Jonas Poole, who travelled to Svalbard five times between 1603 and 1609, brought two polar bear cubs to London in 1609. He presented them to James I, who entrusted them to Philip Henslowe who, with his son-in-law, was 'Master of the King's Beares, bulls and mastiff dogges'.[3] Henslowe had many business interests in Bankside, London's seedy entertainment district. As well as bear- and bull-baiting rings, Henslowe owned theatres that presented works by men with names now sacred to the English literature canon, including Ben Jonson and Christopher Marlowe. His rivals were Richard Burbage and William Shakespeare and their company The Lord Chamberlain's Men. So, on the same day, you might see a play by Shakespeare, visit the polar bears in their own house, and enjoy a bout of bear-baiting. And, in fact, you might see a play and bear-baiting in the same theatre, since Henslowe's Hope Theatre was designed for both. A character in

Polar bears sparring on the tundra.

Ben Jonson's play *Bartholomew Fair*, performed there in 1614, comments that the theatre was 'as dirty as Smithfield and as stinking every whit'.[4] Smithfield once housed cattle pens and has been a meat market since the tenth century. The bear wards were popular figures and the bears had names such as Harry Hunks, George Stone and Ned Whiting. The famous bear Sackerson is mentioned in Shakespeare's *The Merry Wives of Windsor* (1.1). And in *Macbeth*, the beleaguered and fatalistic hero says that his enemies 'have tied me to a stake; I cannot fly,/ But, bear-like, I must fight the course' (v.7).

In 1623 the Spanish ambassador was entertained by a white bear baited by dogs while swimming in the Thames. Two white 'swimming bears' named Mad Bess and Will Tookey were recorded in Bankside ten years later, quite likely the same bears Poole captured.

Stranded on the Thames, 2009, a promotion for Eden, a natural history TV channel.

Paul Friedrich Meyerheim, *Travelling Menagerie*, Germany, c. 1885.

Scholars argue (and argue and argue) whether these bears might have taken to the stage. Certainly there were parts for bears in several plays of the time, but many suggest that these roles were played by a man in a bear suit or, if heavy pulling was required, donkeys in bear suits. We certainly want it to be true that the audience was delighted by the risky addition of a live polar bear or two to a stage play, particularly if it was Shakespeare's *A Winter's Tale*, where a stage direction famously reads 'Exit, pursued by a bear' (iii.3).

The Puritans had all the bears killed in an anti-vice crusade in 1656, sparing only one white cub because it looked so innocent. Perhaps it was the offspring of Bess and Will. Bear-baiting returned with the restoration of Charles ii in 1660. The 'sport' was not made illegal until 1835.

John Oliver, 'View of the Elector of Saxony's Bear-garden, at Dresden in Germany', in Edward Brown, *An Account of Several Travels . . .* (1677).

Royal menageries began to give way to public zoos; the polar bear moved from courtier to commodity that, like other large exotic animals, was used to tempt the public to pay to see them. Perhaps because of their royal origin, however, zoos continue to have a higher status than circuses, although animals can be kept in squalid conditions in both places. Some zoos and aquariums still attract crowds with circus acts or public feedings where the animals 'beg' for their food.

Gradually, zoos began to justify themselves by claiming to be performing an educational mission, which required something more than a series of stinking cages filled with sick and dispirited animals. Germany had begun early to house bears in splendid quarters: an image of the Dresden Bear House published in 1677 shows a group of pampered bears in a large enclosure with climbing posts and a pool. Not surprisingly, then, German zoos led the way, with Carl Hagenbeck's zoo in Hamburg at the forefront.

Rather than putting all the big carnivores in a row, Hagenbeck grouped animals that shared territory in nature in what appeared to be open landscapes. Ditches rather than bars kept the polar bears away from the seals. These enclosures ensured that visitors could see animals apparently wandering freely in a wild landscape. In fact, these enclosures were painted cement stage sets, with cramped cages like theatre green rooms behind. The hard flooring made the enclosures easy to hose out. Although they looked natural, they were far from it.

Hagenbeck had learned his business as an animal dealer from his father, who gave him a collection of seals and a polar bear when he was fourteen. He later conducted expeditions to collect wild animals, which he sold to circuses and zoos and exhibited widely in the U.S. and Europe. Like Henslowe before him, he became an entertainment impresario. In 1909 he brought seventy polar bears to the London Hippodrome, where they performed

Carl Hagenbeck's Tierpark, 'Arctic Panorama', Hamburg, Germany, 1896, postcard.

Abraham Ulrikab's portrait by Jacob Martin Jacobsen, 1880.

twice a day in a show structured around Franklin's quest for the Northwest Passage.[5] At one point the explorer Roald Amundsen discussed a collaboration with Hagenbeck to train bears to pull sledges on expeditions, although this plan never came to fruition. Hagenbeck also played a central role in setting up 'human zoos', where groups of people from distant lands were displayed to the public. In 1880, an Inuit couple from Labrador, Abraham and Ulrike Ulrikab, their small daughters Sara and Maria, their nephew Tobias and another family of three agreed to become an exhibit. Ulrikab was hoping to pay off his debts. They were far from the first Inuit to visit Europe; historian Coll Thrush's account of Inuit visitors to London documents the first Inuit arrival in 1501 or 1502.[6] Ulrikab was a Christian who had been taught by Moravian missionaries to read and write; he kept a diary in Inuktitut during the trip. Their show opened at the Tierpark Hagenbeck on 1 October 1880. Seven thousand people watched as they performed a seal hunt (Tobias played the seal). And of course they were taken to see the polar bears, as a Berlin newspaper explains: 'The Eskimos put the polar bears of the *Zoologische Garten* – which has always been a place of tranquillity – in truly hot excitement. As soon as an Eskimo comes close to its cage, it bursts to the bars in loud grunts and tries to break through them to attack its natural enemy, who he recognizes despite the long captivity.'[7] The recognition of the Inuit by the polar bear demonstrated the 'natural' enmity of the Inuit and the polar bear and their similar 'wildness'.

Ulrikab, depressed by the noise, the bad food and the crowds who broke down fences to get at the families, wrote sadly, 'But here I wait in vain for someone to talk about Jesus. Until now we only saw reckless people in our huts.'[8] The Inuit families had become the respectable equivalent of a circus freak show, their display justified as a contribution to science and public education.

Hagenbeck made the concept of the 'immersion zoo' famous; he displayed animals as if they were in their environmental context. As historian Nigel Rothfels remarks, 'Ever since Hagenbeck, animals have not been collected merely for reasons of science or education, or even really for recreation – animals have been put in zoos increasingly because they are nice, healthy, safe places to be and because the animals, we are told, might be better off there than in the real "wild".'[9]

Carken, Brookfield Zoo poster, Chicago, 1936.

The immersion zoo aims at verisimilitude: *this* is nature. But Rothfels, writing of the history of the modern zoo, argues that such displays 'are fantasies now reinforced by nature television, in which at every turn the camera seems unbelievably ready – and the light implausibly perfect – to catch the most unimaginable shot'.[10] In other words, viewers are still central, however cleverly they are led to believe that a trip to the zoo replicates a trek in the wild.

Zoos have often raised concerns in visitors: 'To a Silver King: A Captive at the Bronx', a poem by Frances Beers which was published in the *New York Times* in 1914, expresses how many people must have felt.

My heart aches for thee, as in thought I see
The dazzling ice fields of thy distant home,
The vast white solitudes where thou didst roam,
The Polar Ocean's dark immensity.
Thou, like thy home, wast lonely, wild, and free;
Who captured thee, in mercy should have slain –
Why have they brought thee here, in heat and pain
To pace the confines of thy cruel cage,
To toss thy untamed head in helpless rage,
To vainly test thy bars, again and yet again?
I cannot watch thee but mine eyes o'erflow
And yet, O captive monarch, well I know,
As these free tears are to that ice-locked sea,
So is my pain to thy dumb agony.[11]

This writing may seem overly sentimental, but its aesthetic quality is not the point. To write directly was unladylike, but women were permitted, even expected, to express emotions that men could not. Newspapers that would not print a woman's letter to the

editor would publish their poems, which gave them a public voice on topical issues.

Beers's poem reflects her close observation of the behaviour that has been called 'zoochosis'. This word describes the mental state – boredom, frustration – that leads some captive animals to produce repetitive movements such as pacing, head-bobbing, or swimming, over and over again, hour after hour. Other individuals may react to captivity with apathy, lying in the same position for hours. Polar bears, along with lions, tigers, wolves and elephants, are particularly susceptible to such behaviour. At one time it was believed that the repetitive pacing of carnivores was tied to their inability to hunt, but a subsequent study showed that the tendency is related to the size of their territories in nature.[12] The larger their territory in the wild, the more likely is the zoochosis. As for 'the heat and pain', polar bears have a hard time cooling themselves, particularly if their enclosures lack shade or a pool deep enough to swim in.

Beers is writing about Silver King, captured and donated to the zoo in 1910 by a rich hunter, Paul J. Rainey. The zoo guide for 1915 comments on Silver King and an adult female: 'Owing to their savage temper neither of these bears ever can be kept with other bears, nor can any keeper ever enter the cage of either. "Silver King" weighs 880 pounds and is probably the largest Polar Bear ever captured alive and unhurt.'[13] Despite Frances Beers's protest, the New York Zoo in the Bronx continued to display polar bears until 2017.

Circuses, perhaps needless to say, are usually worse than zoos for polar bears because travel requires cramped quarters and training often involves physical punishment. Over thirty countries have so far banned the display of wild animals by circuses.[14] The

Inuka, Singapore Zoo, 2015.

Greatest Show on Earth, owned by Ringling Bros. and Barnum and Bailey in the U.S., finally closed in 2017. However, trained polar bears are still rented out for the movie business and displayed as entertainment: a zoo-born female polar bear named Zara was filmed for some scenes of the 2007 movie *The Golden Compass*.[15] Based on the first novel in Philip Pullman's trilogy 'His Dark Materials', part of the story takes place in Svalbard, the kingdom of the ice bears or 'panserbjørn', highly intelligent armoured fighters that resemble polar bears. Apart from Zara, the bears in the film are animatronic. Nowadays it is quite the fashion to rent a life-size animatronic bear for an event. Ironically, they don't do well outdoors in rain or snow (short circuits). However, their

'Capture of Silver King' poster, 1910.

Polar bears in the Washington Zoo, with local entertainers, 1925.

future is bright, given current attitudes to keeping real polar bears in captivity or making them do tricks.

In 1976 Ursula Böttcher, billed as the 'brave, bold, and brilliant baroness of bears', arrived with her ten polar bears; the Greatest Show on Earth had been without a polar bear act for thirty years. Böttcher began her career at the East German Circus Busch. Circuses flourished behind the Iron Curtain as 'people's entertainment', and Böttcher was, strangely, a civil servant. At its peak, her act involved fourteen polar bears and four Kodiak bears. Her favourite bear, Alaska, would 'kiss' her at the end of her show (there was a sugar cube involved). Several of their performances have been immortalized on YouTube. Böttcher's husband was killed by one of the Kodiak bears; nor were the polar bears always tranquil. A fellow performer saw Böttcher come out of a cage with blood pouring down her leg: 'I said, "What happened, are you OK?" . . . Miss Ursula answered, "It was just Neptune, he was playing with me." I said, "Playing with you, are you sure?" She answered, "My dear, if he was not playing with me, we would not be having this conversation."'[16] She gave her last performance, aged 71, in 1998; her remaining polar bears were sold.

In 1996 the story broke that some of her former bears were working in the Suarez Brothers Circus, a Mexican family business founded in 1853 that still tours.[17] The bears often performed in tropical heat and were left in their truck in steamy parking lots. After much agitation, the U.S. passed an act that allowed them to seize the polar bears and send them to zoos. This scandal led to the 2002 passage of a provincial law outlining standards for any institution that received polar bears from Manitoba, one of the main sources of wild-caught bears. Else Poulsen became the keeper of Bärle, one of the rescued bears, and writes an engrossing account of the bear's recovery in *Bärle's Story*. Detroit Zoo's Arctic Ring of Life, completed in 2001 at a cost of about £11 million

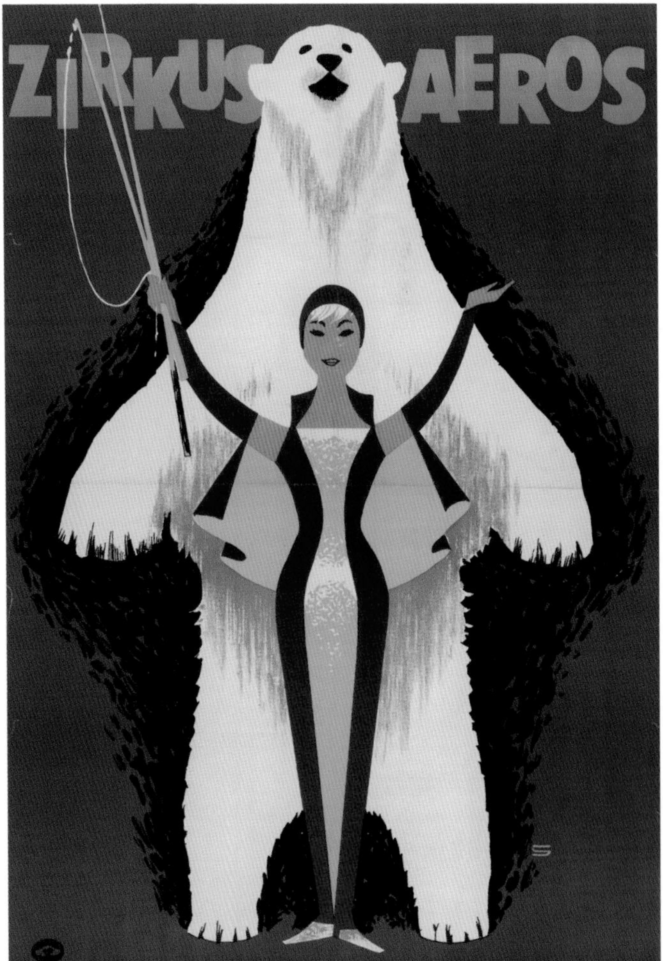
ZIRKUS AEROS

Bear pit, Stanley Park Zoo, Vancouver, c. 1965.

(U.S.$15 million), provided the setting for Bärle's transformation. This small abused bear bravely formed bonds with the other polar bears. Eventually she had a cub, whom she promptly taught to stalk the seals, whose pool was separated from the polar bear pool only by a (fortunately sturdy) wall of Plexiglas. The seals ignored the bears, who spent happy hours 'hunting' them. In order to prevent or minimize the bears' tendency to pace, the zoo provided a constant supply of toys, 'puzzle feeders' and 'furniture', such as piles of tree trunks, to keep them from getting bored. (A favourite bear toy is an orange traffic pylon.) They also had bedding to sleep in and dirt to dig up, which most zoos do not, since the mess takes time and therefore money to clean up.

Few zoos can afford the full-on immersion experience. Ironically, given Silver King's experience, the 1915 *Guide to the New York Zoological Park* comments that, 'To confine large bears singly, in small cages, or in wet-floored, high-walled dungeons, or in the unspeakable "pits" of mediaeval type, is a sin against Nature.'[18] These enclosures provide visitors with an unrestricted view, but the bears are unable to see what they can hear and smell nearby. Many photos show them standing at full stretch, noses in the air, trying to make sense of what is around them. Indoor glass-fronted enclosures, such as those found in some shopping malls, are even worse than the old-fashioned bear pits. Large enclosures completed in the last decade in Detroit and St Louis in the u.s. cost millions. Winnipeg's Assiniboine Park Zoo houses the largest collection of polar bears in North America; its 'Journey to Churchill' exhibit, which includes seals, wolves and muskoxen, as well as a research centre, cost almost £60 million ($100 million Canadian). In response to these costs, some zoos have stopped keeping polar bears. For example, the Smithsonian National Zoo in Washington, DC, made this decision in 1980. London Zoo began to display polar bears in 1829, but stopped in 1985, sending its last polar bear, Pipaluk, to Poland rather than renovate the exhibit. Edinburgh Zoo sent its last polar bear, Mercedes, to a Scottish wildlife park in 2009.[19] And when Gus, Central Park Zoo's 'neurotic' polar bear, died aged 27, and the Bronx Zoo's Tundra died aged 26, both zoos stopped displaying polar bears.[20] Gus was immortalized by Canadian rock group The Tragically Hip in a song titled 'Gus the Polar Bear from Central Park', which repeats the line, 'What's troubling Gus?'[21]

Still, people really like zoos, which were promoted in the English-speaking world by hugely popular early television shows like the BBC's *Zoo Time* (1958–64) and *Zoo Quest* (1954–63), which made zoologist Desmond Morris and broadcaster David Attenborough into household names. In the u.s., *Zoo Parade* (1949–57), featuring zoologist Marlin Perkins, reached an audience of 11 million people in 1952.[22] Around 700 million people visit zoos every year.[23] The

World Association of Zoos and Aquariums (WAZA), founded in 1935, has 250 institutional members and about 1,300 affiliates that belong to regional branches worldwide. However, with an estimated 4,000 licensed zoos and an unknown number of unlicensed ones in the EU alone, this organization represents a tiny minority of world zoos.[24] The others range from large to small, top-notch to squalid. A study of two hundred of the licensed zoos in Europe by the Born Free Foundation (2011) paints a dismal picture, including polar bears kept in small, hard-surfaced enclosures with insufficient drinking water and nothing to do. A study of 24 Japanese zoos published in 2007 concluded that only three of them met the minimum space requirements for polar bears.[25] The Kyoto City Zoo, which opened in 1903, exhibited the polar bears that inspired artist Nishimura Goun.

When Arturo, a polar bear who spent most of his life in the Mendoza Zoological Garden in Argentina, died in 2016, the title of 'the world's saddest polar bear' moved to Pizza, exhibited in Grandview Mall in Guangzhou, China, which holds hundreds of animals, including belugas.[26] In 2017, approximately seventy polar bears were held in thirty accredited Canadian and American zoos.[27] Around thirty polar bears are held by German zoos. But accurate numbers are as hard to find for polar bears in captivity as they are for those in the wild.

Zoos – not to mention world governments – are far from coping with the onrushing wave of extinctions signalled by the IUCN Red List: over a quarter of mammal species are under serious threat. The list signals worse fates for amphibians and seabirds. Yet most species on exhibit in zoos and aquariums are assessed as of 'least concern'. Perhaps, given the treatment of many common species, this is just as well. Much is required of zoos these days. Once they were expected to be concerned with the welfare of the animals and the pleasure of the visitors. Now they are

Nishimura Goun, *Bears* (*Kuma no zu*), 1907–8, one of a pair of six-panel folding screens.

expected to consider how their breeding programmes preserve threatened animals, to contribute to worldwide conservation efforts and to educate the public on how human behaviour is threatening thousands of species. These efforts, however, entail getting humans to grapple with overwhelming problems – habitat destruction, pollution of air, land and water, and climate warming – without simply turning them off.

Some of the same educational experiences that zoos offer are now easily accessed on the Internet, where you can watch documentaries of wild polar bears hunting, mating and just getting around – not to mention happily playing with and then destroying the surveillance cameras designed to film them.[28] But just as people haven't stopped reading books because they have a television, people who look at these videos may be more inclined than ever to visit a zoo or book a cruise to Svalbard. This attraction puts moral pressure on zoos and tourism operators to provide meaningful education programmes about conservation and climate change.

The story of two particular bears – Knut and his mother Tosca – puts some of the controversy over captive bears into context. Their family story inspired a novel: Yoko Tawada's *Memoirs of a*

Polar Bear is narrated in part by Knut's grandmother, a Russian polar bear; then her daughter, the circus bear Tosca, takes over, and finally we hear from Knut, her zoo-born son. These are articulate and literate bears who have opinions about strange human ways.

In the real world, Tosca worked with Ursula Böttcher. Tosca ended up at the Berlin Zoological Garden, founded in 1844, and became notorious as a resistant mother. After abandoning a litter of three cubs, she was bred again and abandoned the resulting twins. Rescued from the exhibit with a fishing net, one cub died and the other became world famous. Knut was the first polar bear in thirty years to survive infancy at the zoo. Immediately a furore broke out about whether it was ethical to hand-rear a bear cub. Death threats flew. Children marched in defence of the tiny bear. Knut survived. The bear and his keeper Thomas Dörflein did two one-hour shows a day between March and July 2007, at which time Knut had become too rough to appear with his keeper. Attendance climbed dramatically. The zoo that owned Knut's father invoked a contract that, it was argued, meant they

Knut and Thomas Dörflein, Berlin Zoo, 2007.

The main gate of the Budapest Zoo, founded 1866, with bears made by the Zsolnay ceramic company.

were owed a share in the profits. Eventually the Berlin Zoo paid €430,000 for Knut. 'Knut' became a trademark and he earned nearly €5 million for the zoo in 2007. Knut's story became the story of a commodity.

Sadly, Knut died of encephalitis, aged four, in 2011. He fell into a pool during a seizure and drowned in front of hundreds of visitors. There is no way to measure what all the emotion poured into his life and death did for the fight against climate change, the justification given by the chairman of the zoo board of trustees for his short existence.[29] Else Poulsen, with a darker viewprint, likens walking through this zoo to 'touring a cemetery full of memorial mausoleums', which she sees as the explanation not only for Tosca's abandonment of her cubs, but for her incessant pacing.[30] Many zoos like this one, which has heritage buildings dating from the nineteenth century, are prevented by law from replacing them. Few have the expansive grounds that would allow the bears enough space in which to roam.

What are the justifications for the captive breeding of polar bears? Polar bears born in captivity cannot be reintroduced into

Global Seed Vault,
Svalbard, 2008.

the wild, since their survival depends on two to three years of seal-hunting experience with their mothers. In an article intended to dampen enthusiasm for captive breeding as a solution to extinction, Noel Snyder and his co-authors note that despite a few well-known success stories, captive breeding is a poor option for most species. Further, the promise of captive breeding can give 'a false impression that a species is safe so that destruction of habitat and wild populations can proceed'.[31] However, they also see zoos as 'one of the major hopes for the conservation of biodiversity' and support captive breeding to 'ensure supplies of animals for exhibition'.[32] And despite the difficulties, between 1978 and 2002 an estimated 1,000 polar bears were born in captivity.[33] As Knut's story reveals, both the costs and rewards of displaying polar bears are high.

Some argue for captive breeding as a way to maintain a diverse genetic pool. A small wild population destined to be drastically reduced by melting ice will become inbred. This goal would

require the zoos holding polar bears to collaborate on a breeding programme, a project that would require around two hundred bears.[34] Then wild females could be artificially inseminated. This type of response to the predicted loss of genetic diversity – whether through climate change, nuclear disaster or asteroid strike – lies behind the Global Seed Vault, aka the 'Doomsday Vault' in Svalbard, Norway. Several 'frozen zoos', including one at the San Diego Zoo, cryopreserve eggs and sperm from endangered species. However, none of these plans really deal head-on with the fact that wild polar bears need ice to survive.

Some situations perhaps justify zoos keeping polar bears. Orphaned cubs likely to fall victim to wolves or larger bears in the wild are given a home in zoos. Other zoo bears such as Bärle have been rescued from circuses or other zoos. Without zoos, these bears would die or have to be euthanized. Attempts have been made to keep orphan cubs in the wild: a study conducted in the 2000s to see if female bears in Manitoba with one cub would foster a second ended in failure.[35] Some in Churchill protested the recent removal of two cubs to the zoo in Winnipeg, arguing that a study should be done to see how they manage.[36] Agonizing questions arise at every turn.

Polar bears do a lot to reward visitors to zoos where they are happy, proving that if we entertain them, they will entertain us. The question is: how do zoos connect to conservation efforts in the wild? How do we return the gift of the polar bear?

Polar bears have featured not only in zoos and circuses, but in museums. Like zoos, museums began as elite collections that gradually opened to the public. Both originally displayed their specimens in what would seem today like an odd jumble, however glorious. 'Wonder rooms' or 'cabinets of curiosities' were the pride of collectors; they contained art, curios and exotic artefacts, and items of natural history such as minerals, shells, antlers and taxidermied rare animals. Automatons or medical curiosities might be included. One of the most famous collections, put together by the Danish doctor and collector Ole Worm in the early seventeenth century, had a stuffed polar bear hanging from the ceiling. Worm catalogued his collection and used it to correct long-standing misconceptions, for example, that narwhal horns came from unicorns. However, these collections were intended as much to convey status as to educate. They originally inspired curiosity, awe and envy. The rich men who were able to buy live bears often had them taxidermied when they died, so the bears could continue to radiate an aura of power and wealth, often in an entrance hall, acting as majestic guardians. When the family downscaled,

where else to send the polar bear but the museum? In a project that crosses art and archive, *nanoq: flat out and bluesome*, Bryndís Snæbjörnsdóttir and Mark Wilson set out between 2001 and 2004 to find, photograph and catalogue all the taxidermied bears in the UK. Some still stand in stately homes; others are crammed into storage. This project led to a beautiful book and an exhibit of ten of the 34 bears they discovered. Displayed in clear Plexiglas cases without labels, the bears seem to float. The result is haunting. The project did more than discover objects, however. In the book, part-catalogue and part-critique (with contributions by several others), Snæbjörnsdóttir and Wilson trace a cultural network that filled museums and stately homes with polar bears. In moving

Ole Worm's cabinet of curiosities, frontispiece to *Museum Wormianum* (1655).

these bears out of these contexts through photography and the final exhibition, they force a rethinking of how human activities impact nature. But they don't tell us what to think: 'No solutions are presented, only suggested associations that cannot help but resonate.'[37] However, perhaps the haunting comes from the realization that we, and the polar bears, have moved into a different world since the bears died or were killed, one where we need to reconsider our relationship.

Just in case you are (still, after all this) wondering how to find polar bear items for your stately home or for that special gift for a visiting head of state, a quick visit to the web produces many options: a bronze polar bear by François Pompon for £60,000; a full-sized taxidermied polar bear for £30,000; and a white stone carving of a polar bear by the late Lukta Qiatsuk, an Inuk

Taxidermied bear in Tromsø, Norway, 1960s.

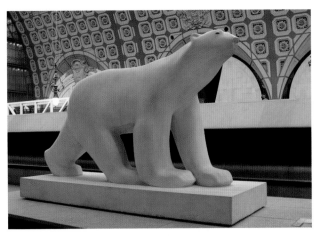

François Pompon, *Polar Bear*, 1929, stone.

from Cape Dorset, for £8,000.[38] Polar bears remain popular for porcelain and jewellery designers and others who craft items for the luxury trade. Although perhaps not quite as impressive as a taxidermied polar bear, rugs do put that finishing touch to the salon beside the fireplace or the grand piano.

Control over large exotic animals and beautiful women stands in for power and control over nature, land and resources. As Julia Emberley has shown in *The Cultural Politics of Fur* (1997), fur was regulated by European sumptuary laws aimed at preventing the lower orders from dressing above their station. Ermine (the name for the winter coat of Arctic weasels) trimmed the royal robes of monarchs (polar bear fur would have been too coarse and too hot). A woman in furs was like a wild animal, her sexuality untamed. *Venus in Furs* is a novel by Leopold von Sacher-Masoch (1870), the man whose name was used to describe a sexual orientation. His cruel Venus wraps herself in dark 'despotic' furs that set off her white skin.[39] The tradition of depicting women in various degrees of undress on fur rugs had already become a cliché by the time

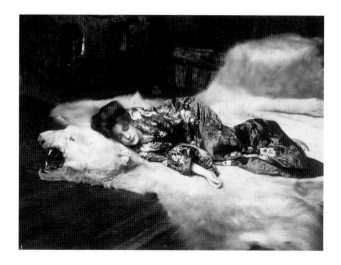

Elinor Glyn turned up to write her scandalous novels and screen-plays. One wit wrote:

> Would you like to sin
> With Elinor Glyn
> On a tiger skin?
> Or would you prefer
> To err with her
> On some other fur?[40]

Glyn, born in 1864, somehow managed to transcend childhood years spent in Upper Canada to become a famous romantic novel-ist and scandalous socialite. Allusions to Glyn are common: Evelyn Waugh has a character in his novel *Men at Arms* (1952) reciting the verse about her when he sees a polar bear rug in a London club.[41] Marilyn Monroe is the most famous of the many actors and film stars who have posed on polar bear rugs: a perfect symbol of sex and wealth combined. Among others was Evelyn Nesbit, who moved from artists' model to fashion model, chorus girl, cover girl and one of artist Charles Dana Gibson's 'Gibson Girls'. Her beauty led to 'the murder of the century' when her unstable millionaire husband murdered the playboy who had drugged and raped her as a young teenager. Needless to say, her reputation suffered more than anyone else's after this shocking event.[42]

It is not only the rich and famous who find polar bears attractive. For the not-so-upscale set, toy polar bears in a variety of shapes and sizes abound, although clearly other species of bear still have an edge. Winnie-the-Pooh was named after a black bear; Paddington is an Andean bear; even Rupert started out brown and only went white to save ink.[43] And polar bears have been domesticated for other human purposes. Even toddlers (especially toddlers) are quite familiar with talking animals who promote everything from online banking to breakfast cereal. What is called mascot marketing uses memorable 'spokescharacters' imbued with positive emotions. Mascots appear at tourist promotions and sports events such as the Olympics. Coca-Cola, the world's largest beverage company, started using polar bears in its branding in 1922.

These brand mascots appeal to the toddler in all of us. Who can resist smiling at a penguin in a TV ad waddling around clutching its mobile phone? Anthropomorphized and animated charismatic megafauna wear clothes, live in houses, have names and drink Coke. Reducing once ferocious polar bears to a commodity as a pelt, a rug or a work of taxidermy has not been enough; we have also made them cute. Cuteness, an aesthetic category tied to commodification, has led to the worldwide production of toys with big eyes and soft round bodies in Europe, North America and, in particular, Japan. If you insert 'polar bear' into the eBay search box, you will find 'cute polar bear hijab pins', 'marshmallow polar bear' and 'cute mochi squishy bears'. Cuteness denotes 'an

Seducing a polar bear, advertisement for Anis del Oso by artist René Lelong, c. 1930.

aesthetic of accentuated helplessness and vulnerability' based on 'an exaggerated difference in power'.[44] According to theorist Sianne Ngai, 'In its exaggerated passivity and vulnerability, the cute object is as often intended to excite a consumer's sadistic desires for mastery and control as much as his or her desire to cuddle.'[45] This impulse, in fact, is implicit in the idea of biting into

sweet food like marshmallows and sticky Japanese mochi cakes. Perhaps unsurprisingly, the Coca-Cola bear is now appearing as a sales-mascot at Walt Disney World, huge but unthreatening, adorably cute.

Sacher-Masoch and Ngai both suggest the link between power differences and cruelty, a link that might lead to questions about keeping animals in cages for public viewing or the apparently benign desire of some scientists to prevent the extinction of polar bears by controlling their reproductive lives. An early take on this fantasy is found in Mary Shelley's *Frankenstein*. Dr Frankenstein usurps Nature's – some would add God's – power of creation. Later he refuses the desperately lonely Creature any chance to have a mate. The Creature retaliates, killing Frankenstein's bride on their wedding night and taking her place as the focus of Frankenstein's emotions: their relationship sinks into violent, compulsive hatred. The emotional lives of the two characters become deeply, creepily entangled in ways that lead to death for both of them.

In *The Child Garden* (1989), science fiction novelist Geoff Ryman engages this theme with the clear intent of taking it apart and reworking long-standing gender and species categories and hierarchies. Milena, the main character, falls in love with Rolfa, a genetically engineered woman who is part polar bear, part human, originally designed for mining in Antarctica. Rolfa composes an opera based on Dante's *Divine Comedy*. Somehow, despite Milena's inability to understand that Rolfa is singing not for humans but for viruses, their love moves them and the world through purgatory, beyond time and self. In *Frankenstein*, the ending is tragic, even apocalyptic; in *The Child Garden* it is comic. What will it be for us?

5 It Takes Two to Tangle

Y'know, polar bear is so intelligent! You go out and you
hunt, and if you don't use your head and the knowledge
you got, he'll outsmart you. And I've seen it happen
time and time again.
Roger Kuptana, Sachs Harbour, Inuvialuit Settlement Area[1]

Although even the thought of encountering a polar bear face to
face can evoke heart-pounding terror, the long-standing reputation of the polar bear as a man-killer is overblown. In Churchill,
Manitoba, on Hudson Bay, where at some times of year the bear
and human populations are almost equal, serious work has
been done to effectively reduce human–bear conflict. Commercial
hunting took bears in increasing numbers starting in the early
eighteenth century. Serious declines in polar bear numbers led
to the Agreement on the Conservation of Polar Bears in 1973. This
and other agreements have required the production of more scientific knowledge about the bears, in particular their population
sizes and trends (up, down, stable). The push to conserve wild
animals by nation states and such international organizations as
the World Wildlife Fund / World Wide Fund for Nature and
Greenpeace has led to pressure on Indigenous hunting communities. Important and, unfortunately, sometimes acrimonious
conversations about polar bears include bureaucrats, polar bear
scientists, Indigenous hunters and conservationists.

Although the invention of the high-powered rifle and snowmobile have made the hunt into an 'arcade shooting game',
stories of polar bear attacks on humans get more attention than
do human attacks on polar bears.[2] The Inuit and explorers generally killed polar bears in self-defence or for food; however, for

whalers, polar bear pelts supplemented their income from whales and seal products. As early as 1750, London had 5,000 street lights powered by whale oil; whale oil and baleen became major trade items over the next century and a half. Svalbard became the site of busy whaling ports and 'manufactories' where whales were butchered and the blubber processed. By the 1820s, the bowhead whales were nearly extinct in the waters around Svalbard and Greenland.[3] Whalers moved west to places such as Herschel Island in the Beaufort Sea, where they significantly reduced the bowhead population.[4] Whalers from California, New England and Europe killed polar bears mainly for their pelts: as Ian Stirling points out, 'Over 6,500 whaling voyages in Davis Strait, Hudson Bay, and Baffin Bay [were made] between 1719 and 1916.'[5] The Hudson's Bay Company traded around 15,500 pelts prior to 1935; and whalers, mostly non-Indigenous, killed an estimated 40,000 polar bears, the majority between 1890 and 1920.[6] The total harvest in Eurasian polar areas (Siberia and Svalbard) from the 1700s to 1969 has been estimated at 150,000.[7] And 'between 1871 and 1973, over two thousand polar bears went to

On the skyline, polar bear in Arctic Alaska.

zoos, carnivals and vaudeville theatres all over the world'.[8] Hunting continued after these dates, when snowmobiles and ski planes made killing polar bears easier. A particularly diabolical device was the set-gun, which consisted of a baited box containing a loaded rifle with the trigger attached to a piece of bait, which when bitten and pulled on by a bear shot it in the head.

In contrast to these centuries of slaughter, polar bear attacks are few, although often fatal. Our narcissism supports the belief that bears are supremely focused on killing and eating humans, although given a choice they would always pick a nice fat seal. Polar bear expert Tom Smith comments: 'People talk about polar bears stalking and hunting humans. If that's the case, they're doing a pretty poor job of it.'[9] An academic study published in 2017 reports: 'From 1870–2014, we documented 73 attacks by wild polar bears, distributed among the 5 polar bear Range States (Canada, Greenland, Norway, Russia and the United States) which resulted in 20 human fatalities and 63 human injuries. We found that nutritionally stressed adult male polar bears were

Seamen on the Whale fishery killing a Polar Bear

Samuel Howett, 'Seamen on the Whale Fishery Killing a Polar Bear', c. 1785, pen and brown ink.

most likely to pose threats to human safety.'[10] Unfortunately, two Inuit men were killed in Nunavut by polar bears in 2018, one in July near Arviat, and one in August near Naujaat (Repulse Bay).

The depiction of the polar bear as inimical to humans started early in Euro-Western accounts; in his *Synopsis of Quadrupeds* (1771), Thomas Pennant describes their behaviour and appearance quite accurately, but emphasized their preference for 'human bodies, which they will greedily disinter: they seem very fond of human blood; and are so fearless as to attack companies of armed men, and even to board small vessels'.[11] Although the Comte de Buffon remarks that polar bears 'never fail to dig up dead bodies', he also notes that the polar bears 'who arrive with the ice on the coasts of Iceland or Norway are starved to such a

140

degree, that they devour every thing they meet, which may have given rise to the prejudice, that these sea-bears are more fierce and voracious than the common kind'.[12] The human imagination can far outdo anything that a real bear can manage. Here is James Hogg in 'The Surpassing Adventures of Allan Gordon' (1837) purporting to represent the views of Christian Greenlanders:

> Man and woman continued to aver that these animals never yet invaded a settlement in that country that they did not devour every bone of its inhabitants before they left it . . . They represented them as liking best to eat children alive and that in order to enjoy such a meal with perfect zest they always held the children down with one paw and began at the feet and eat upward and that the poor things would be crying and trying to creep away even when the monsters had proceeded leisurely with their meal nearly as far as the heart. Then they affirmed that they ravaged all the women and then suck their blood from the throats.[13]

Unusually, in a natural history published in 1774, Oliver Goldsmith describes polar bears as 'naturally a timorous animal'.[14] In 1785 David Thompson saw at least a dozen polar bears a day during his walk from Churchill to York Factory with two Cree guides. He was surprised by how lethargic the bears were. His guides advised him to walk by quickly without looking; only one even bothered to growl.[15]

In fact, polar bears are not as fierce as other bears; smaller but more aggressive grizzlies routinely chase polar bears off whale remains in Kaktovik.[16] A Russian who crashed in the sea between Canada and Greenland in 2015 while trying to fly a helicopter around the Arctic Circle(!) was able to scare three polar bears off his ice floe before rescuers found him.[17] On Wrangel Island, Nikita

Ovsyanikov, armed only with a stick and an attitude, discovered he could walk safely through dozens of hungry polar bears waiting for the ice to form.[18] Still, no expert discounts the possibility of an unprovoked attack. The Inuit sense of the danger of polar bears is reflected in stories of the huge ten-legged polar bear called Kokogiak, formerly hunted by now-vanished giants.[19] Mitiarjuk Nappaaluk's novel *Sanaaq*, written in Inuktitut syllabics in the early 1950s, describes the near-panic of her strong heroine on encountering a polar bear. It is understandably difficult to remain calm when a large, curious and hungry carnivore is ambling towards you, even if it has only four legs.

Else Poulsen, the zoo bear specialist, argues that the 'over-emphasis on the predatory quality of bears has done more to

John Ross, 'A Polar Bear Plunges into the Sea', 1819, engraving by R. Havell & Son.

hurt the animal than any other single factor in history'.[20] Part of the problem has been the tendency to exaggerate the danger faced by Arctic explorers, thus enhancing their heroism – an exaggeration sometimes indulged in by the explorers themselves, sometimes by those who have aimed to tell an inspiring story of national courage.

François-Auguste Biard, *Fight with Polar Bears*, 1839, oil on canvas.

Other representations are designed to titillate an audience with gruesome depictions of violence. For example, consider the *National Geographic* video about Churchill, 'Polar Bear Alert', that aired on television in 1982. The narrator intones that the town is the 'one place in the world where the great white bears roam the streets, dangerously immune to the presence of their only enemy: man'.[21] After interviews with townspeople about scary encounters with bears, one of the show's producers is shown on the tundra in a rebar cage: 'Next comes a harrowing point-of-view sequence of polar bears rattling, pummeling and chewing the thing.'[22] This same producer had made a documentary in 1971 that featured shots taken from an underwater cage of great white sharks swirling in the bloody waters near commercial whaling boats. His documentary provided inspiration for Peter Benchley's best-selling novel *Jaws* (1974), later made into a blockbuster movie. Benchley later regretted his depiction: 'I couldn't possibly write *Jaws* today . . . not in good conscience anyway. Back then, it was generally accepted that great whites were anthropophagus (they ate people) by choice. Now we know that almost every attack on a human is an accident: the shark mistakes the human for its normal prey.'[23] However, the temptation to depict animals in attack mode is hard to resist. In 2013 the BBC produced 'incredible footage of BBC cameraman and [a] hungry polar bear' by putting the cameraman inside a Plexiglas cage filming a polar bear trying to get in.[24] Of course the cameraman was in no danger, given that people in skidoos, just out of camera range, were ready to chase the bear off. Polar bears are always hoping for food, but this hope is mixed with a general curiosity that impels them to check out new things in their otherwise rather blank landscape.

Rather than attacking people out of sheer inherent viciousness, polar bear attacks usually arise out of their situation (startled, starving, protecting cubs, in pain, sometimes from gunshot wounds) or human behaviour (walking alone at night when bears are around, feeding bears, sometimes to lure them into camera range, camping with food nearby, for example). A surprising number of people, mostly young men, have been killed after they have jumped into polar bears' zoo enclosures.[25] In 1994, in the Anchorage Zoo in Alaska, Binky the polar bear injured two tourists who intruded on his space to take his picture. Perhaps Binky should have been named Wrathful or Fang? Zoos now spend as much time thinking about keeping people out as keeping bears in. They should also reconsider their naming practices: at the Philadelphia Zoo a female polar bear who lived to the age of 37 was named Coldilocks.

When the Agreement on the Conservation of Polar Bears was negotiated in 1973, Canada, Greenland and the U.S. pushed to allow for continued hunting 'by local people using traditional methods in the exercise of their traditional rights and in accordance with the laws of that Party'.[26] What 'traditional methods' consist of has not been well defined. Quota-based subsistence hunting provides food where imported meat is prohibitively expensive. In many remote communities, the only way to get goods from the south, including staples, is by air. In Nunavut, many families do not have enough money for food.[27]

For people living in the Arctic, meat, particularly seal meat, has always been a staple. Only a few wild plant foods, like berries and seaweed, are part of Arctic diets. Unlike seals, whales or caribou, polar bears have never been a primary food source, but they do provide meat for people and dogs, and skins for rugs and clothing. Inuvialuit elder Pat Ekpakohak of Ulukhaktok remarked that polar bear skin makes excellent mitts and trousers: 'The hair doesn't fall off like caribou skin . . . Polar bear pants last 20 years or 30 years or more.'[28] Apphia Agalakti Awa of Pond Inlet remembers a fortunate kill:

Of course there was no selling polar bear skins then, so it was all ours. It was a very fat polar bear. We used the fat to light the qilliq [stone lamp]. There was not much meat around the camp at that time, so my father-in-law cut the meat up and divided it equally among the people in the camp. There were some people who were very poor and hungry . . . When Kalirraq got the polar bear we stopped being hungry. We were eating polar bear meat – we were happy.[29]

A primary difference between the beliefs of non-aboriginals and Indigenous hunting cultures in North America is that many Indigenous people believe that humans do not control the hunt: animals do.[30] In fact, for Indigenous people a hard border between animal and people does not make sense: Mary Kamoo-kak (Gjoa Haven) says, 'The first polar bear was a human that turned into a polar bear. That is where we believe they came from.'[31] Many Inuit believe that provided the bodies of animals

Bob Knights hunting seals on polar bear skin from the floe edge, Sachs Harbour, 1958.

killed for food are properly treated in ritually respectful ways, they are an infinitely renewable resource.[32] Obviously, scientists and bureaucrats do not agree; for them, animals can and should be managed by humans. The Inuit respect for animals, however, does not mean that they cannot be killed and eaten. In 1975 Peter Okpik, an Inuk from Gjoa Haven, said: 'A person is born with animals. He has to eat animals. That is why animals and a person are just like one.'[33] The Greenlandic-Danish explorer Knud Rasmussen noted the Inuit belief that

Polar bear looking up, Svalbard, Norway.

> Animals have in reality no objection to being killed by human beings, as long as the rules of life are observed by the latter. It may even happen and not infrequently, that an animal will approach a human being, actually desiring to

be killed by that particular person. An animal may perhaps be tired of being what it is; and since its soul cannot change its envelope until the body has been killed, it is natural that animals should sometimes wish to die.[34]

The idea that animals offered themselves was part of a larger set of beliefs that required everyone to share food and to respect others, including animals. Thus to refrain from killing an animal that offered itself risked insulting it, which might bring bad luck in hunting, even starvation, to one's community. Whatever others think of these beliefs, they underpin part of what it means to be Inuit. This relationship between hunter and prey is presented as emotion-laden, familial and profoundly reciprocal. This viewpoint contrasts with the dominant one that sees humans as on the culture side of the nature/culture binary and thus, because of their superior knowledge, in charge of animals. Nonetheless, most people, Indigenous or not, believe that humans have a responsibility to keep polar bears from suffering or dying out.

As in many other Indigenous stories about animals, polar bears transform into humans and back into bears, marry humans, adopt humans and provide humans with food. In one Inuit story a man marries a polar bear. He wins a life-or-death contest with the largest polar bear in the village of his new parents-in-law by obeying the instructions of his mother-in-law without question.[35] Humans, clearly, have much to learn from animals. In another story, an old woman who can barely keep up with her family finds herself confronted by a polar bear. She turns her mittens inside out, puts them on the end of her stick and thrusts it between the bear's jaws, choking it to death. Triumphant, she hobbles into camp to share the good news of a feast. She rides on the sled from then on.[36] Both stories emphasize the power of older female figures.

Child and polar
bear cub, 1940s,
Anglican Diocese
of the Arctic.

To successfully hunt a polar bear remains an important rite of manhood for Arctic peoples, and polar bear trousers are a sign of status.[37] *Nanook of the North* (1922), a film made by Robert J. Flaherty, has often been dubbed the first documentary.[38] Allakariallak, a hunter from Port Harrison (now Inukjuak) who played Nanook, was crucial to the success of the film, which combines fiction (the two women in the film were not his wives) and fact (the walrus hunt with traditional weapons was not staged).

Allakariallak, star of the documentary *Nanook of the North* (Robert J. Flaherty, 1922).

What was staged were a few comic scenes; in one Nanook is mystified by a record player, although Allakariallak was as familiar with record players as he was with hunting rifles. Flaherty, Allakariallak and their team almost starved looking for a polar bear to film.[39] In the end the polar bear appears only in the form of Nanook himself, named after the bear, his beautiful polar bear trousers and a tiny polar bear he makes out of snow so that his little boy can practise using his bow.

A few women still hunt polar bears, too. An Inuvialuit hunter from the western Canadian Arctic, Roger Kuptana, recalls, 'In the older days, those women were just like men – just as tough and strong!'[40] In other locations, however, such as Arviat on Hudson Bay, women did not hunt polar bears. There, some people felt that the quota tags should be reserved for young men.[41]

Traditionally, a variety of rituals surrounded the killing of a polar bear in different places in the circumpolar Arctic, such as waiting a certain number of days before killing another polar bear, facing the bear's head in a certain direction and hanging gifts on or around it.[42] Even if these rituals are no longer followed, hunting polar bears facilitates the transmission of land-based knowledge between generations as well as providing meat and income.

Getting trapped on a moving ice floe while out hunting polar bears has always been a danger in some areas. As ice conditions are changing rapidly, traditional knowledge based on experience travelling over the ice is ever more important. The risk of falling through the ice on a snowmobile is much greater than with a dog team. John Max Kudlak remembers:

> I started hunting polar bear with my granddad. He wouldn't let me shoot anything until he knew I knew about the ice and the current. Everything to do with polar

bear, I had to learn the ice conditions first, the movements, and then after I learnt all that he'd stop and ask me, 'What's going to happen now?' . . . It took me three or four winters just to learn about the ice until my granddad said, 'You know enough, you can go out and hunt for yourself.' He didn't want me going out and never coming back. He was telling me all these danger signs – what's going to happen, how you can walk on the ice. The young ice could be anywhere from a foot to four inches. He was a real good teacher. He could tell stories in the night time about when he was drifting out on moving ice and how to get back when you're drifting on the floe edge.[43]

Nunavut and the Northwest Territories permit sport hunting within the subsistence quotas. This hunting requires a local Inuit guide and must be conducted on foot or by dogsled. Communities are assigned a quota: the number of bears residents are permitted to hunt. Hunters must attach the official tag that proves their right to hunt a bear to the pelt of any bear they kill.[44] Any bear killed in self defence in a community is subtracted from the quota, and if the quota is already filled, it is taken from the quota for the following year.[45] Tags are usually distributed by lottery and the winner has the right to transfer the tag to someone else in the community or sell it to a sports hunter or outfitting company. The number of tags sold for sport hunting varies greatly between communities, but before 2008 was usually less than 20 per cent of the quota. Sport hunting, mostly by u.s. hunters, has decreased since 2008, when the polar bear was listed as 'threatened' under the Endangered Species Act and the importation of trophies into the u.s. was banned.[46] That the percentage of sport hunting is so low reflects the value community members place on reserving the hunt for themselves. Nor is all sport hunting successful (one survey put the success rate at about 55 per cent).[47] The tag from an unsuccessful hunt cannot be transferred: 'Once you've sold a tag to a sports hunter it's gone, whether he gets [a bear] or not. Most of the time, the sports hunters they're looking for a big animal, so even though they see small ones, they never shoot.'[48] A guided sports hunt can bring up to $30,000 Canadian into a community, supporting not only the primary guide but young assistants as well, who thus learn how to survive out on the land. Although any meat goes to the community, pelts are not used as much for clothing now as in the past and are sold. Currently, polar bear rugs are selling for retail prices between $15,000 and $35,000 Canadian.[49] Notably, all these activities are regulated at many levels from the local to the international.

What is called the 'management harvest' includes bears shot in self defence, mercy killings and the removal of 'problem bears'. These are subtracted from hunting quotas. The setting and enforcing of quotas sometimes involves multiple overlapping national and regional jurisdictions. The best up-to-date and detailed summary of estimated polar bear numbers, changes in break-up and freeze-up dates ('sea-ice metrics') and 'human-caused removals' can be found on the website of the Polar Bear Specialist Group of the IUCN. Under 'human-caused removals' can be found the potential removals (hunting quotas) and the actual removals both for the past five years and the past year.[50] Morten Joergensen, a tourist expedition leader, argues in *Polar Bears on the Edge: Heading for Extinction while Management Fails* (2015) that uncertainty about numbers means that legal hunting in the U.S., Canada and Greenland, combined with suspected poaching in Russia, is unsustainable. This statement is rather broad. The situation of polar bears varies greatly between subpopulations; hunting is a threat in areas where the numbers are declining: Western Hudson Bay, Southern Hudson Bay and the Beaufort Sea.[51]

Climate change does mean that reproduction rates and, therefore, what counts as sustainable hunting will change as well. However, in a recent article, Eric Regehr and others argue that the traditional harvest rate of 4.5 per cent for polar bears is sustainable provided half as many females are killed as males; uncertainty about numbers, resilience and ice conditions are taken into account; and 'a state-dependent management framework' is followed.[52] In fact, 'Harvest levels in 2015–16 were less than 3.4% of the estimated Canadian polar bear population of 16,560 bears.'[53] Those that call regulated hunting, including sport hunting, 'conservation hunting' do so for a reason. Lands that support hunting are seen as more valuable and are less likely to be opened for development. Regulation enforces bans on hunting females with cubs, as well as other rules on how the hunt is conducted. Furthermore, Indigenous hunters have reduced quotas voluntarily in the past.[54] The 1988 Inupiat-Inuvialuit agreement that manages hunting in the Southern Beaufort Sea population was developed as a voluntary 'Native to Native' agreement.[55]

Some Indigenous elders worry that the quota system is changing their relationship to bears: 'We never thought of killing a whole lot of bears before. But when you start to impose something, people want to do it more. So when the laws came in prohibiting people from shooting a bear, everyone wanted to do it. Leave people alone and they'll be conservative.'[56] These elders are well aware of the scrutiny from the south that dictates that if they 'change their way of life to one that is less traditional, they begin to lose the moral advantage based on the value of preserving such a traditional life'.[57] Traditional beliefs about hunting developed when it was not intensive enough to endanger animal populations; hunters were few and widely spread out. Now, human populations are larger and increasing and animal populations are under pressure from climate change, pollution and

development. Nor was there a cash incentive to hunt as there is now. However, forces outside Indigenous control, including state and international regulations, mean that hunters sometimes face the alternative between ethics and eating. They are not the only ones who should be asked to consider the impact of their actions.

Polar bear skin on a qamutik, Cape Dorset, Nunavut, 1999.

Those in the animal rights and conservation movements are beginning to consider to what degree they themselves are 'part of a continuing colonial process in the Canadian North'.[58] Small, remote communities that have relied on the fur trade and subsistence hunting for hundreds of years have few economic options. The hunt for seal pups off Newfoundland became the target of activists in the 1970s. Bans on importing seal products such as the 2010 EU ban and campaigns against wearing fur severely affected Inuit incomes, even though they hunt adult seals in sustainable numbers. Tanya Tagaq, an internationally famous

Inuit throat singer, has pointed out how easy it seems to be for animal rights activism to arouse widespread ire against Indigenous hunters instead of – say – McDonald's.[59] Presumably, animals bred for slaughter are seen as already dead, whereas for modern city dwellers, exotic and distant wild animals have lives that are seen as ever more valuable as their numbers diminish.

The way the Inuit hunt polar bears has remained much the same over many decades. Franz Boas, known as the father of American anthropology, began his career studying the Inuit on Baffin Island in the winter of 1883–4. Boas explored and mapped much of the coasts of Cumberland Sound and Davis Strait by dog team. He writes: 'The Eskimos pursue [polar bears] in light sledges, and when they are near the pursued animal the traces of the most reliable dogs are cut, when they dash forward and bring the bear to bay. As the hunter gets sufficiently near, the last dogs are let loose and the bear is killed with a spear or with bow and arrow.'[60] An Inuvialuit man, Nuligak, born on the Mackenzie Delta in 1895, writes somewhat sadly after the Second World War, 'Today the Inuit are unfamiliar with this method of hunting bears with dogs. They can no longer recognize the distinctive tones of the barking when a nanuk is at bay.'[61]

However, *Hunters of the Arctic*, published in 1966, gives a very similar description of the hunt. The authors, who were making a documentary, worked with a dog team run by David and a snowmobile run by Idlout, both from Resolute Bay: 'We had almost lost sight of the bear, which was a long way ahead; it went straight over obstacles we had to find our way around and seemed likely to escape us. David bent forward and cut the traces of two huskies. They darted off, barking furiously.'[62] When the hunters had almost given up, the two dogs came back. Yelping and barking, they encouraged the other dogs and the hunters to follow them to where the bear was at bay. Roger Frison-Roche notes in *Hunters of the Arctic* that the Inuit hunters could tell how long ago a track was made, and if the meat was infested with parasites.

One advantage of dog teams is that they don't break down (although snowmobiles are more reliable now, Idlout spent a lot of time doing flying repairs) and another is that if hunters are forced to stay on the ice overnight, the dogs warn them if a polar bear comes close. Dogs also can find their way home through fog or blizzard. And, if all else fails, hunters can eat dogs to survive. At the time this last hunt was conducted, dog teams were under threat from distemper and from the Royal Canadian Mounted Police, who were enforcing regulations against allowing dogs to wander, often shooting them without any consultation or compensation. Although this was couched as a public safety measure, it led to the near-extinction of the dogs and the end of much of the nomadic hunting that had supported most Inuit families.[63] The bitter memories of that time were aired at the Qikiqtani Truth Commission, which reported in 2010.[64]

Inuit polar bear hunting is often represented by outsiders as purely an economic activity nowadays, yet old beliefs and techniques still persist. In an account of a 1979 polar bear hunt, geographer George Wenzel notes that

> hunters consistently stated that the polar bear was fully as intelligent as a human being and that it understood when it was being ridiculed or belittled. On the 42 polar bear hunts I observed while in the eastern Baffin area, virtually every hunter reminded me never to joke about bears because to do so would bring future misfortune in polar bear hunting.

After the 1979 hunt, he wondered aloud why the bear foolishly let the snowmobiles approach so closely. The two young men butchering the animal stopped their work to warn him not to criticize

the bear; later the hunt leader warned him again, but added that since Wenzel 'was a white man it probably would not have any serious effect'.[65]

Polar bears are usually pretty solitary and, where possible, stay out on the ice year round. A great deal of research on polar bears comes mainly from the southernmost populations of bears on Hudson Bay. Because the ice in Hudson Bay always melts in the summer, these bears are forced onto land, which leads to the potential for human–bear conflict, but also to the opportunity for scientific research and for many delighted tourists and web-cam viewers to watch the bears in their natural habitat. Churchill, Manitoba, labels itself 'the Polar Bear Capital of the World' for good reason. The town is situated near the area where the ice forms first, as a result of the counter-clockwise currents and west-erly winds that force the newly formed ice from the rivers north of there onto the coast. Maps show a notch about a third of the way down the Manitoba shoreline: this is Cape Churchill. As the ice piles up in this notch, polar bears muster – waiting to be able to go out hunting seals – as do the tourists, watching the bears from school buses and tundra buggies.

The human population of Churchill in 2016 was around nine hundred. Churchillians are outnumbered at various seasons by outsiders – some human tourists, some birds and mammals. The melting of the ice brings polar bears to land in July. At this point, many head inland where they hang out in dens dug in the peat moss to stay cool and shelter from flies. Once the temperature drops below freezing around the end of October, most start moving towards the coast. The exception is pregnant females, who den inland too, some as far as 100 km (60 mi.) inland.[66]

Other hot spots for polar bear–human interaction are Svalbard (pop. 2,700), an archipelago governed by Norway, and Barrow

A polar bear tests the strength of thin sea ice.

(Utqiagvik) and Kaktovik, on the north coast of Alaska, where the remains of butchered whales are left as far from the villages as possible because they attract furry visitors. Wrangel Island and Herald Island, northeast Chukotka, Siberia, are thought to have been the last refuge of the woolly mammoth; they are also major polar bear denning sites.[67] In September 2017 Finnish cruise ship passengers observed around 230 bears on Wrangel, feeding on a beached bowhead whale.[68] Until recently, Wrangel Island was a strict nature reserve, but in 2014 a military base was built there to secure strategic Arctic sea routes for Russia.[69]

Compared to other locations where bears congregate, Churchill is accessible. It was a research and rocket range starting in the mid-1950s. The u.s. Army had a base there until 1970 and Canada continued to use it for research into the upper ionosphere until 1985. Tourism really did not ramp up until the 1980s, but scientists

Polar bears scavenge on the garbage dump outside Churchill, Manitoba, Canada.

began work there in 1966, when the Canadian Wildlife Service hired Chuck Jonkel to begin field studies of polar bears. When he arrived in Churchill, the soldiers on the rocket range routinely fed the bears, as well as providing a serious amount of rubbish for them to explore. Once the range closed, these bears moved into refuse dumps in Churchill where they became a spectacle for locals in cars. Distressed by the number of bears being shot, he helped invent bear spray, made commercially available around 1990, and worked on developing safer and more effective tranquillizer darts. Jonkel was also motivated to reduce the danger to people in Churchill, which had been inadvertently founded on a polar bear migration route when the railway was completed there in 1929.

Tommy Mutanen was killed by a polar bear in 1983 in the ruins of the recently burned Churchill Hotel after getting meat out of a freezer. He ran into a bear in the dark, attracted by the meat. Mutanen was a Sayisi Dene, one of a group moved into Churchill from the interior in 1956 by the government at short notice and with no consultation:

Unable to hunt for food because government officials feared that they would kill too many moose and caribou, many of the Dene were forced to go to one of the dumps in the area to find their supper: 'You got along with polar bears so long as you didn't dig in the same pile or fight over the same piece of meat.'[70]

Mutanen's death, along with the near-fatal mauling of a photographer the same year, led to many changes in how Churchill approached the management of polar bears.

Usually human–bear conflict arises over food: campers' backpacks and coolers, household waste and town dumps are objects of desire for bears. Once a bear has found food in a particular location, it will come back, becoming what the experts describe as a 'food-conditioned bear'. As Sherry Simpson points out in regard to brown and black bears in Alaska, we move into their territory, leave food out for them (rubbish, pet food, bird seed in feeders) and then wonder why they become problem bears. In the end, we find ourselves killing wildlife to protect rubbish.

A polar bear named Linda, not yet two years old, turned up in the Churchill dump on her own in 1966.[71] She had learned to forage there from her mother and taught several successive pairs of her own cubs to do the same. She made it clear that bears not only remember where food can be found, but pass this information along. This discovery heightened the importance of preventing

Holding facility, Churchill, Manitoba, painted by Kal Barteski.

bears from ever associating food with human beings. One polar
bear that happened across a shed containing a moose carcass (oh
joy!) subsequently specialized in knocking over sheds whether
they had anything edible in them or not.[72]

Churchill has put a great deal of thought into polar bear deter-
rence, in part because it increasingly relies on tourism. The town's
'Polar Bear Alert' programme encourages villagers to call in bear
sightings and the Manitoba Conservation or Canada Parks officers
respond, hazing the bears with their vehicles and air-horns or, on
foot, with shotguns loaded with cracker shells that flash and bang,
or with rubber bullets.[73] Bears that do not move along are tranquillized and installed in the building popularly known as 'polar
bear jail'. The holding facility has 28 cells including two with
air-conditioning. Because the goal is to avoid any association
between humans and food, the bears (who would be fasting

anyway) are all given water, but only mothers with cubs are fed. To reduce any habituation to humans, interactions are kept to a minimum. The live traps around town now set off a signal when they are triggered so that conservation officers can quickly check to see if vulnerable cubs have been left outside. Eventually, bears in the holding facility are tranquillized again and moved by truck or helicopter further north or out on to the ice. The result has been that the number of bears euthanized has decreased markedly from 1976, when 29 bears were killed, to fewer than one bear a year.[74]

Such a programme makes economic sense only where there are many polar bears on land where they may run into people. Elsewhere, the locals are more vulnerable and intruding bears are usually shot. Churchill was lucky in that it could repurpose military buildings to house the bears and the rubbish and that it had the infrastructure to support tourism, including the roads that are now patrolled by tundra buggies rather than tanks.

Attitudes in Churchill have changed considerably from a time when polar bears were viewed as dangerous vermin or late-night entertainment. The shift from military base to a location where scientific research and tourism fuel the local economy has meant a much more thoughtful approach to human–polar bear relationships. However, if polar bear numbers continue to decline in the area, tensions between hunters and the tourism industry will mount.

6 Save the Polar Bears!

You shouldn't underestimate the power of a star.
A star can influence society, maybe even more than
a politician. I dream someday that Knut will be like Joan
of Arc, holding a huge SAVE THE EARTH banner in his hand
and leading a massive demonstration.
Knut's veterinarian in Yuko Tawada's novel *Memoirs of a Polar Bear* (2014)[1]

To the nineteenth-century discourse of the polar bear's exotic ferocity, the twentieth century added one of vulnerability and cuteness. As climate change grew harder to ignore, however, the polar bear began to symbolize a death far wider than the prospect of its own extinction. One reaction to this future has been denial. Another has been called 'pre-emptive mourning', where images of starving or dead polar bears draw viewers 'into the melancholic space of the already extinct polar bear'.[2] Activists and scientists hope to inspire the public to grapple with climate change, now threatening the ice on which the polar bear depends. Circumpolar peoples would like a voice in these discussions, which risk ignoring their interests today as much as in the heyday of imperialism. Blake's balanced 'fourfold vision' is perhaps more necessary now than it was at the beginning of the modern period, which many see as the beginning of the Anthropocene – the geological period marked by permanent human-caused changes to the planet's earth, air, ice and water.

Ian Stirling, a leading polar bear scientist, has this to say about the threat of climate change:

The deep and widespread attraction to polar bears, felt even by people who will never see one in the wild, translates directly into human understanding that the long-term effects of climate warming on the planet as a whole are likely to be devastating. The simple clarity of this understanding is anathema to climate-change deniers, but may be the most significant contribution that polar bears can make to the overall well-being of humans and the planet as a whole.[3]

Certainly, many humans aim to save the bears, and perhaps the polar bears will help save us. As the twenty-first century began, polar bears surged to the fore in debates about threats to the Arctic ecosystem. The polar bear became an icon of climate change or, as one popular analogy had it, the canary in the planetary coal mine. Al Gore, famous for his unsuccessful run for the U.S. presidency in 2000, has long worked to focus public attention on climate warming. His 2006 documentary *An Inconvenient Truth* included an animation of a polar bear trying to climb on to a disappearing ice floe: 'In the year following its May 2006 opening, [the film] garnered the third highest box-office receipts of any documentary in history.'[4] That same year, the cover of *Time* magazine featured a polar bear with the caption, 'Be worried, be very worried.'[5] In 2007 Leonardo DiCaprio, a climate activist and film star, appeared on the cover of *Vanity Fair*. Gazing adoringly up at him is a polar bear cub, a star in his own right, the Berlin Zoo's Knut. The irresistibly cute Knut gazes up at the equally cute DiCaprio, posed by celebrity photographer Annie Leibovitz in a way that would have satisfied the Romantic painter Caspar David Friedrich.[6] The struggle to get the polar bear listed as threatened under the U.S. Endangered Species Act succeeded the following year. However, the secretary of the Interior stated, 'Despite his acknowledgement that the polar bear's sea ice habitat is melting due to global warming, the ESA will not be used as a tool for trying to regulate the greenhouse gas emissions blamed for creating

climate change.'[7] Still, the campaign focused public attention on the issue, which was the point. Models of climate change and sea ice can be eye-glazingly boring (Bayesian statistics, anyone?), but the polar bears made the danger real. After all, they are the most charismatic of a wide range of animals similarly threatened, including ice-dependent seals and walruses.

Backlash was quick. According to Spencer Weart, 'The number of items on the internet that connected global warming with the words "hoax", "lie", or "alarmists" more than doubled just between January 2008 and January 2009.'[8] Polar bears focused the debate between those who believe human activities are contributing to climate change and those who do not. Ten years later, nation states, scientists, academic institutions and many industries have reached a consensus that the human production of greenhouse gases contributes to global warming and that this warming will

Polar bear sprawling on thin Arctic Ocean ice.

seriously impact all life on the planet. Almost 70 per cent of Americans believe that 'global climate change is happening'.[9] World opinion agrees, although concern is weaker in the countries that emit the most greenhouse gases.[10] The UN Framework Convention on Climate Change (1992) led to the Kyoto Protocol (1997) and the Paris Agreement (2015), with almost all nations agreeing that human-produced greenhouse gas emissions cause global warming. Those who disagree are a small but often well-funded minority.

In both Europe and North America, large amounts of corporate funding have been funnelled, often covertly, to 'think tanks' that spread uncertainty about climate warming. The funders use the methods that tobacco companies developed to stall the regulation of smoking. This history is recounted in *Merchants of Doubt: How a Handful of Scientists Obscured the Truth on Issues from Tobacco Smoke to Global Warming* (2010) by Naomi Oreskes and Erik M. Conway. China emits more greenhouse gases than any other nation on an absolute basis, but far less on a per capita basis than the top three per capita emitters (Canada, then Australia, then the U.S.) and about the same as the EU.[11] Since these democratic countries emit more greenhouse gas than China, perhaps it is only fair that they should also suffer most from the anxiety and acrimony surrounding open discussion of the issue, not to mention the difficulty of enacting effective laws.

How is the struggle going? Unlikely as it might seem, at least one person has seized on the popularity of polar bears in ways that forward the argument that climate change is a hoax. If you search for polar bears on the Internet, you likely will come across Susan J. Crockford's blog. Crockford, an adjunct professor of anthropology, runs a private company that identifies bone and shell fragments for biologists and archaeologists. She is also a sharp thorn in the side of the IUCN's Polar Bear Specialist Group.

She calls the best-known polar bear scientists the 'usual go-to guys for *polar-bears-are-all-going-to-die* media frenzies'.[12] In fact, not even the most pessimistic polar bear scientist predicts extinction for the polar bear in the foreseeable future. Stirling suggests a small population might well survive in the Canadian archipelago for an indeterminate period.[13] The IUCN Red List predicts a decline of 30 to 50 per cent of the world populations in the next 35 years, however, which is bad enough.[14] It does not help that polar bears have a long generation time (fifteen years), a low reproductive rate and a high infant mortality rate (only about one-third of cubs make it to two years).[15]

Crockford's very first 2012 blog post, 'Cooling the Polar Bear Spin', begins:

> I've had quite enough of the obfuscation of facts and model-based extrapolations into the future with regards to polar bears. I'm pretty sure I'm not the only one who is interested in what polar bears are doing **now** . . . Spare us the emotional media hype, icon-peddling and fear-mongering about the future – we'd just like some information about the bears![16]

As she begins, so she continues, her claims made in frequent posts in her down-to-earth and occasionally vituperative style. In the world she creates, scientists and journalists spread lies to a naive and gullible public, lies that only she can correct.[17] As she promises, she produces a (selectively) fact-filled site about polar bears, but it is by no means unbiased. Her position is that polar bears are doing just fine. Her argument goes this way: the evidence that led to listing polar bears as 'threatened' under the U.S. Endangered Species Act predicted steep declines in summer sea ice by 2050, with polar bear numbers falling sharply in tandem. However, the

drop in summer sea ice in 2007 was much greater than the model predicted. Indeed, she claims, it matched the 'steep declines' predicted for 2050. With this decline, polar bear numbers were predicted to plummet by more than 30 per cent and possibly up to 67 per cent with ten subpopulations disappearing altogether.[18] However, polar bear numbers remain fairly stable. What happened? First, the polar bears proved to be better at the increasingly long fast between break-up and freeze-up than expected. Second, despite Crockford's claim, the actual decline in ice coverage in 2007 was far less than the loss predicted for 2050. Steven Amstrup, one of the authors of a 2007 article repeatedly cited by Crockford to make her point, refutes it directly. He says, 'according to the National Snow and Ice Data Center, the average September sea ice extent for the years 2007 to 2017 was 4.5 million square kilometers, "nowhere near the low levels projected it would be by the middle of the century."' He continues: 'To say that we already should have seen those declines now when we're not nearly to the middle of the century yet is absurd.'[19] If Crockford grants that ice levels in 2007 were much higher than they are projected to be in 2050 her argument collapses.

Some would see major ice loss as a sign that the scientists were right about global warming, if wrong about polar bear resilience. Crockford turns the argument around: if polar bears are OK when scientists said they wouldn't be, then we can't trust scientists. And, she implies, we can't trust the consensus about global warming either. Her unstated argument is that if the polar bears are all right, so is the planet, a move a paper critical of her blog calls 'climate-change denial by proxy'.[20] This is the spin that makes her useful to the Heartland Institute in the U.S., the Global Warming Policy Foundation in the UK and others who deny climate change.[21] As far as she is concerned, 'the polar bears have been saved'.[22] Her sunny optimism makes polar bear scientists look like deranged worrywarts.

In fact, the future that Crockford wants us to ignore has already arrived for the most southerly populations around Hudson Bay and in the Beaufort Sea.[23] There, as the ice declines, so will the bears, however gradual the changes seem now. Polar bears are good at fasting, but not immortal. When females cannot hunt enough between March and June to sustain a pregnancy, birth rates will fall. The IUCN Red List reassessed the polar bears' future in 2015 and continues to list them as 'vulnerable'. Even Crockford has recently admitted that 'polar bears may be negatively affected by declines in sea ice some time in the future – particularly if early spring ice loss is significant'.[24] Much of the debate between polar bear scientists and Crockford has been about summer sea ice, perhaps distracting attention from the point that bears do most of their hunting and eating between March and June. What the polar bear scientists are saying is that the increasing loss of summer sea ice will inevitably become loss of spring sea ice, which will in turn negatively impact the bears and their seal prey. Because this change has been occurring gradually, the situation of the polar bear is much like that of the frog in the pot of water being brought, ever so slowly, to a boil. A gradual decline in numbers suddenly can become a population crash.

The discourse that could be labelled 'the plight of the polar bear' may not, in fact, provide the ideal framing for climate change education, given that it privileges one species not only over the Arctic ecosystem as a whole, but over the people who live in close quarters with polar bears. Nuancing the discourse at this point may be difficult, given public interest. A video produced by *National Geographic* in December 2017 of a dying polar bear is estimated to have been seen by 2.5 billion people, which is about two-thirds of the world's population with access to the Internet. *National Geographic* subtitled the story 'this is what climate change looks like'. There were varying responses:

> Many people expressed gratitude that we'd shined a light on climate change, but others angrily asked why we had not fed the bear or covered him with blankets or taken him to a vet – none of which would have saved him . . . And then there were those who are still bent on maintaining the dangerous status quo by denying the existence of climate change. We became to them yet another example of environmentalist exaggeration. But they offered us a glimpse of the daunting number of people we still need to reach.[25]

Because no one could say just what was wrong with that particular polar bear (it swam away), *National Geographic* revised the video, commenting, 'While science has established that there is a strong connection between melting sea ice and polar bears dying off, there is no way to know for certain why this bear was on the verge of death.'[26]

Some have moved to calling the Arctic the planet's air conditioner, hoping this metaphor will resonate better.[27] This move appropriately widens the issue to the Arctic ecosystem rather than one species. However, this metaphor depicts the Arctic as a utility for southerners: 'our' air conditioner. Arctic residents would like to have *their* human rights recognized too, as outlined in a 2015 memoir by Inuit politician and Nobel Prize nominee Sheila Watt-Cloutier, *The Right to be Cold*.

The representation of Indigenous lands as an 'empty' resource free for southerners to exploit is a colonial one. Few remember that in 1946, as the Cold War ramped up, Canada offered what is now Wapusk National Park, a major polar bear denning site just south of Churchill, to the U.S. and the UK as a test site for twelve Hiroshima-sized bombs. The plan argued that timing would allow prevailing winds to send the fallout north, and only 'the occasional hunter or trapper' would be affected. Fortunately the area was deemed too cold for the scientists and the project moved to Woomera, Australia, where the traditional owners of the land were relocated.[28] The Russians moved Indigenous people and their reindeer from Novaya Zemlya in order to conduct nuclear tests between 1955 and 1990; U.S. nuclear testing took place in Alaska between 1965 and 1971 against the protests of the Aleut people and many others.[29] The Arctic continues to be treated as a resource for southerners rather than as a homeland for northerners, including polar bears.

Oil and gas promoters, nature tourists and eco-activists make strange bedfellows, but they all have often acted as if no one whose opinions might matter lives in the Arctic. The power of numbers and money explain this real or feigned oblivion. For example, the luxury cruise ship *Crystal Serenity*, which holds over 1,700 passengers and crew, accompanied by its own icebreaker and helicopters, recently began to bring tourists north to see rare Arctic wildlife. So instead of Carl Hagenbeck's project of taking animals and people from remote areas to urban centres to entertain the locals, now those from urban centres are arriving to see remote peoples and wildlife. The power differential between the two groups remains just as large as it was in the nineteenth century. Dealing with the carbon footprint and accident risk of such cruises will become harder as they proliferate, which they will.[30]

Arctic residents have specialist knowledge that might help find solutions. They report more polar bears arriving in their communities than in the past, contrary to the scientists' numbers. Adamie Delisle-Alaku, Nunavik, says: 'We do acknowledge climate change. We are the ones living it the most. But we're not talking about climate change. We're talking about polar bears.'[31] Do increased sightings mean more polar bears or just more polar bears forced off the melting ice coming into villages looking for food? Those calling for stricter quotas or even a ban on hunting may have the numbers correct, but they often fail to consider how hunters and communities can be properly consulted and compensated and how to support the continuation of cultural teachings around hunting.

Frank Pokiak, from Tuktoyaktuk, points out that Inuit hunters have longer memories of polar bears than the scientists: 'It's really not recognized that we had knowledge of these things from our parents . . . It's something brand new only because scientists are saying it.'[32] Roger Kuptana from Sachs Harbour notes: 'The way of doing science and traditional knowledge is so far apart – the way of thinking, the way of doing things. It's hard to say, but I do know that what the scientists are doing – studying polar bears – isn't harming the polar bears and is doing us a lot of good, you know!'[33] Andy Carpenter, also from Sachs Harbour, says that scientists 'know just about as much as us! Both the scientists and the hunters, they could help each other. Once you start sharing information with different people, it's always very interesting and things start happening.'[34]

And interesting things are happening. The IUCN now takes Traditional Ecological Knowledge (TEK) into account in producing its population estimates. The members of Hunters and Trappers Organizations (HTOS) have detailed knowledge of their local areas, and some scientific studies have depended on it.[35] Organizations like Greenpeace and the WWF have adopted policies mandating consultation and collaboration after realizing that some of their past campaigns ended up hurting Indigenous communities. Governments are involving Indigenous people in policy discussions. For example, five communities (Pond Inlet, Arctic Bay, Grise Fiord, Resolute Bay and Clyde River) worked on the development of the Lancaster Sound Marine Conservation Area (2017).[36] And several writers argue that TEK could be even better integrated into scientific research and policy development. For example, women are a good source of information on polar bear health, as one hunter points out: 'Here probably everyone has an opinion on polar bear health, but it would probably have to be the ladies that do all the fleshing [who would be really knowledgeable about polar bear health]. They see the marks and . . . how much fat or blubber's left on them.'[37] This is local environmental knowledge held by those who work closely in particular locations with polar bears, which can be of considerable use, particularly when integrated with the knowledge of scientists who may be in the Arctic for shorter periods, but who coordinate their knowledge across the circumpolar region through collaboration, conferences, journal publication and similar academic activities. This integration is difficult when scientists and Indigenous hunters disagree, perhaps an inevitability given the differences between their respective worldviews and economic situations. An anthropologist who studies hunting cultures, Paul Nadasdy, comments:

> Because scientific managers can only make use of certain types of knowledge about animals (those that can be expressed quantitatively or graphically, such as population figures and distributions), a great deal of hunters' knowledge (all the stories, values, and social relations that transmute those animals from a set of population figures into sentient members of the social, moral, meaning-filled universe of the hunters) 'drops out of the database' as irrelevant.[38]

Resolving the differences between polar bear scientists, bureaucrats tasked with protecting polar bears, Indigenous hunters, anthropologists, people living in the circumpolar north, promotors of northern development and the hugely engaged southern general public is certainly not easy, particularly given the ways in which polar bears spark controversy in the political debate around climate change.

Polar bear scientists and wildlife defenders are not the only ones who have used polar bears to get a message across. Mascots, usually abstracted, cartoonish and 'cute', were originally chosen without considering that the habitat of the real animal may be under threat from the same companies using it as a brand. For example, Coca-Cola is currently the subject of a Greenpeace campaign to reduce single-use plastic bottles that end up in the oceans. On the other (green) hand, Coca-Cola HBC – a leading bottler of Coca-Cola – has committed to a science-based target to reduce its emissions by 50 per cent per litre of drink by 2020.[39] And further, spurred by the threat to its brand mascot posed by the warming

Carlton the bear, the Toronto Maple Leafs mascot, at the Toronto Film Festival, 2016.

planet, Coca-Cola has committed to raising £7.5 million (U.S.$10 million) over five years for the WWF to protect a refugium, a place where the remaining unmelted ice will collect surviving polar bears. The project is, rather sadly, called 'Last Arctic Home'. It includes the entire Canadian Arctic archipelago, the north Baffin Bay region including Lancaster Sound, the area north of Greenland, parts of Siberia, and the Bering Strait, which separates Russia from Alaska.[40]

Certainly, the right mascot conveys a powerful wordless message. Saving the polar bears requires protecting the Arctic ecosystem which, in turn, requires tackling not only greenhouse gas emissions, but the other threats posed by pollution, particularly from oil and gas exploration and production. In 2012

March of the polar bears, protest of Arctic drilling at the White House, Washington, DC, 2013.

Greenpeace, spurred on by the Deepwater Horizon oil spill in the Gulf of Mexico in 2010, started its 'Save the Arctic' campaign. The Deepwater spill went on and on, eventually dumping almost 5 million barrels of oil into the Gulf, twenty times more than the 1989 Exxon Valdez tanker grounding in Alaska, which permanently damaged a pristine environment. Greenpeace has mastered the art of getting public attention. Let's face it, dressing up as a polar bear is always fun: the campaign featured hundreds of polar bears waving signs in front of Shell stations, not to mention the White House.

In 2014 Greenpeace tackled an arrangement between Shell and Lego dating from the 1960s. Lego had long produced kits bearing the Shell logo that encouraged children to build tanker trucks, petrol stations and even oil rigs. Lego ended its relationship with Shell that same year. The next year, Greenpeace parked a giant animatronic polar bear named Aurora outside Shell's London headquarters, along with her attendant ice floes. Film star and screenwriter Emma Thompson spoke from atop the bear. A month later, Shell announced an end to its Arctic exploration as too expensive and too risky.

The following year, the WWF took Shell to court (using funds from Coca-Cola) to argue that its exploration licences granted in Lancaster Sound in the early 1970s had expired. Shell Canada voluntarily relinquished them. This move opened the way for Lancaster Sound to be declared a national marine conservation area. Cynics might see these concessions as related to the low price for oil in these years, but public concern for polar bears certainly played a role. Norway and Russia continue oil and gas development in their Arctic waters, however, and pressure continues in Alaska. Russia has recently built a string of new military bases across its Arctic islands, including one on Wrangel Island and another in Franz Josef Land, both important polar bear territory.[41]

The WWF also has been leveraging the power of public art to further its cause. Danish artist Jens Galshiøt, supported by the WWF, produced a sculpture titled *Unbearable* for the Paris climate summit in 2015. A life-sized copper polar bear is impaled on an oil pipeline that follows the curve on a graph of carbon emissions,

Polar bear installed by Greenpeace outside Shell's office, London, 2015.

with its dramatic rise beginning in 1850. WWF, Nokia, Panasonic and local community groups also supported the Ice Bear Project of British artist Mark Coreth. He created three life-size bronze polar bear skeletons that are covered with ice sculpted to form the bear's body. When the temperature rises, the ice melts, revealing the skeleton beneath. One sculpture was unveiled at the

Jens Galschiøt, *Unbearable*, a life-sized copper polar bear impaled on an oil pipeline, Paris exhibition, 2015.

Copenhagen climate summit in 2009 and they have been displayed in London, Toronto and Montreal.[42]

Another project, a film called *It's the Skin You're Living In*, directed by David Harradine, begins with a shot of a polar bear walking in a stunning landscape of snow and ice.[43] Then he takes off part of his polar bear disguise, exposing his human head and arms to the bitter cold. A hybrid creature, he walks first in the Arctic, and then along busy highways, and finally arrives home to make a cup of tea, still wearing his grubby and unravelling costume. The film conveys a sense of the combined menace, ordinariness, sentimentality and wonder involved in human–polar bear relations, and the quandary that we, and they, are in. This activist art hits at the emotions to amplify the force of scientific arguments that not everyone has the time or patience to absorb.

If we return to the polar bear on the ice floe with which we began, we are still left with an array of disparate human reactions. Some embrace denial (the bears are fine) or pre-emptive mourning (the bears are dying, and sadly, nothing can be done). Many Indigenous people respect the bear as an other-than-human person, while others value it as an irreplaceable and sentient part of a complex ecosystem. Other responses assert human control: tranquillizing bears, moving orphan cubs to zoos, considering captive breeding and artificial insemination. Still others value the prestige of personal access to a scarce resource: non-Indigenous hunters display their trophies and tourists display their photos.

The history of the polar bear and its human entanglements certainly explains the impulse to seize the moral high ground in attacks on other humans who appear to endanger polar bears, including capitalists, climate change deniers, oil and gas companies, rich tourists, zookeepers and even Indigenous hunters. A focus on saving the polar bear may distract us from wider and far more intractable problems or ease guilt about other entanglements

– our love of cars, plastic, air conditioning and other modern marvels. The planet is suffering from a constant drive for resource extraction to fuel development and the paired insistence that the (human) birth rate must be kept up in order to keep consumption high and the economy running.[44] Blake would see this argument as Newton's 'single vision' run amok. Some way of balancing human needs with those of polar bears and other creatures must be found. After all, the planet can and will go on without us and without polar bears, too. Rather than fabricating glorious visions of technological rescue or sinking into apocalyptic despair, we could salvage some species-respect by trying to repair some of the huge damage we have done to the planet in the past, a much humbler project. Wilderness campers are invariably instructed to pack out their own rubbish, and perhaps this simple principle might serve as a start.

Timeline of the Polar Bear

EST. 400,000 YEARS AGO	8,000 YEARS AGO	450 BC–AD 1250	AD 985
Polar bears diverge from brown bears	Hunters kill polar bears on Zhokhov Island, Siberia	Palaeo-Eskimo Dorset people carve polar bears from walrus ivory and soapstone	The Norse settle Greenland and trade polar bears and their pelts with northern Europe

1670	1774	1845	1925
Hudson's Bay Company founded; polar bears enter the North American fur trade	Constantine John Phipps publishes the first scientific description of *Ursus maritimus*	John Franklin's expedition departs in search of the Northwest Passage	Svalbard, prime polar bear habitat, comes under Norwegian control

1973	1975	1992
Agreement on the Conservation of Polar Bears signed by the range states	Convention on International Trade in Endangered Species of Wild Fauna and Flora (CITES) formed to control international trade in endangered species or their products	United Nations Framework Convention on Climate Change (UNFCCC), signed by all UN member states

1252	1594	1609

Henry III of England receives a polar bear from Haakon IV of Norway

Dutch explorer Willem Barentz and crew encounter polar bears in Svalbard

Two polar bears arrive in London, gifts for James I

1948	1961	1968

Founding of the International Union for the Conservation of Nature (IUCN)

Founding of the World Wildlife Fund for Nature / World Wide Fund for Nature (WWF), now the world's largest conservation organization

IUCN establishes the Polar Bear Specialist Group (PBSG) composed of scientists from each of the five polar bear range states: Canada, Denmark (Greenland), Norway (Svalbard), the Soviet Union (Russian Federation) and the U.S.

1999	2006	2010

Founding of Polar Bears International, a non-profit polar bear conservation organization

Al Gore's *An Inconvenient Truth*, a documentary on global warming, features an animated polar bear struggling to climb on to a melting ice floe

Polar bear genome sequenced in draft

References

INTRODUCTION

1 Charles Foster, *Being a Beast* (New York, 2016), p. 120.
2 See Species at Risk Public Registry, www.canada.ca, accessed 11 February 2018; IUCN Red List of Threatened Species, www.iucnredlist.org, accessed 19 February 2018.
3 See Alethea Arnaquq-Baril's documentary *Angry Inuk*, National Film Board of Canada, 2016.
4 Languages and Cultures, www.polarbearsinternational.org, accessed 23 October 2018.
5 William Blake, *Blake: Complete Writings*, ed. Geoffrey Keynes (Oxford, 1969), p. 818.
6 John Leslie, *Narrative of Discovery and Adventure in the Polar Seas and Regions: With Illustrations of their Climate, Geology, and Natural History* (New York, 1831), p. 65.
7 Jon Mooallem, *Wild Ones: A Sometimes Dismaying, Weirdly Reassuring Story About Looking at People Looking at Animals in America* (New York, 2013), p. 25.
8 Zac Unger, 'Polarizing Bears: How Environmentalists and Skeptics Misrepresent the Science on Polar Bears', https://thebreakthrough.org, 9 June 2014.
9 Olaudah Equiano, *The Interesting Narrative of the Life of Olaudah Equiano, Or Gustavus Vassa, The African* (London, 1789), p. 215.
10 John Ross, *Narrative of a Second Voyage in Search of a North-west Passage* (London, 1835), p. 248.
11 Michelle Theall, 'Alaska Whale Hunt Keeps Polar Bears Alive', www.sierraclub.org, 9 June 2018.

12 I use the term 'Inuit' to refer to the peoples of Arctic North America, although they are not culturally or linguistically homogeneous. Otherwise I use 'Indigenous' or 'circumpolar peoples' for generalizations about these groups, although these terms are sometimes imprecise.

13 'Languages and Cultures', www.polarbearsinternational.org, accessed October 2018.

14 Quoted in 'Nanuq', in *Canada's Polar Life*, ed. P.D.N. Herbert and J. Wearing Wilde, www.polarlife.ca, 2002, accessed 19 February 2018; these quotations are from the Igloolik Oral History Project (IOHP), which is a collection of more than four hundred interviews with Inuit elders from Igloolik.

15 Vladimir Randa, 'Uumajunik uqaruluujaqtuq, "speaking badly to/about the animals" or How Human Speech Affects Them', in *Orality in the 21st Century: Inuit Discourse and Practices*, ed. B. Collignon and M. Therrien (Paris, 2009), p. 6.

1 EARLY ENCOUNTERS

1 Al Purdy, 'Lament for the Dorsets', in *15 Canadian Poets Plus 5*, ed. Gary Geddes (Toronto, 1978), pp. 62–3.

2 S. Liu et al., 'Population Genomics Reveal Recent Speciation and Rapid Evolutionary Adaptation in Polar Bears', *Cell*, CLVII/4 (2014), pp. 785–94.

3 As with polar bear origins, genetic studies and new fossil finds keep shifting the dates of human origin.

4 Andrew E. Derocher, *Polar Bears: A Complete Guide to their Biology and Behaviour* (Baltimore, MD, 2012), pp. 9–10.

5 C. Leah Devlin, 'The Letters between James Lamont and Charles Darwin on Arctic Fauna', *Polar Record*, 51 (2015), p. 496.

6 'The Red Bears: The Cave Art Paintings of the Chauvet Cave', www.bradshawfoundation.com, accessed 15 February 2018.

7 See Margarita A. Kir'yak (Dikova), *The Enigmatic World of Ancient Graffiti: Rock Art in Chukotka, The Chaunskaya Region, Russia*, trans. Richard L. Bland (Oxford, 2015).

8 'Ekainberri: The Replica of the Ekain Cave', www.ice-age-europe. eu, accessed 12 January 2018.

9 Vladimir V. Pitul'ko and William W. Fitzhugh, *The Zhokhov Island Site and Ancient Habitation in the Arctic* (Vancouver, 2013), p. 110.

10 Matthew W. Betts, Mari Hardenberg and Ian Stirling, 'How Animals Create Human History: Relational Ecology and the Dorset-Polar Bear Connection', *American Antiquity*, LXXX/1 (2015), pp. 89–112.

11 See Keavy Martin, *Stories in a New Skin: Approaches to Inuit Literature* (Winnipeg, 2012), pp. 20–36. Recent genetic studies indicate that the Dorset (Tuniit) did not intermix with the Thule (ancestors of the Inuit); see Maanasa Raghavan et al., 'The Genetic History of the New World Arctic', www. sciencemag. org, 29 August 2014. Quoted in *Uqalurait: An Oral History of Nunavut*, comp. and ed. John Bennett and Susan Rowley (Montreal, 2004), p. 143.

12 Victoria Dickenson, *Seal* (London, 2016), p. 60.

13 Snorri Sturluson, *Heimskringla*, vol. 1, trans. Alison Finlay and Anthony Faulkes (London, 2011), p. 10.

14 George M. Durner et al., 'Consequences of Long-distance Swimming and Travel over Deep-water Pack Ice for a Female Polar Bear during a Year of Extreme Sea Ice Retreat', *Polar Biology*, XXXIV/7 (July 2011), pp. 975–84.

15 'Killing Polar Bears in Iceland "Only Logical Thing to Do"', http://icelandmonitor.mbl.is, 18 July 2016; see also Alexander Stubbing, 'Polar Bears in Iceland: An Overview, History and Proposed Response Plan', thesis, Master of Resource Management, University of Akureyri, Iceland, 2011.

16 Medieval Mapping Project, 'Audun in the Western Settlement', www.uvic.ca, accessed 20 February 2018.

17 T. J. Oleson, 'Polar Bears in the Middle Ages', *Canadian Historical Review*, XXXI/1 (March 1950), p. 49.

18 Quoted in Michael Engelhard, *Ice Bear: The Cultural History of an Arctic Icon* (Seattle, 2017), p. 36.

19 Oleson, 'Polar Bears', p. 50.

20 For a translation of the story, see William Ian Miller, *Audun and the Polar Bear: Luck, Law, and Largesse in a Medieval Tale of Risky Business* (Leiden, 2008).

21 Daniel Hahn, *The Tower Menagerie: Being the Amazing Story of the Royal Collection of Wild and Ferocious Beasts* (London, 2003), p. 21.

22 Richard H. Russell, 'The Food Habits of Polar Bears of James Bay and Southwest Hudson Bay in Summer and Autumn', *Arctic*, XXVIII/2 (1975), p. 127.

23 Alice French, 'How the Thames Went from "Biologically Dead" to Full of Seals', www.timeout.com, accessed 3 March 2018.

24 Hahn, *The Tower Menagerie*, p. 43.

25 Mary Refling, 'Frederick's Menagerie', A Conference Paper Read at the Second Annual Robert Dombrowski Italian Conference, Storrs, CT, 17–18 September 2005, http://faculty.fordham.edu, accessed 19 February 2018.

26 Marco Polo, *Travels of Marco Polo*, ed. Peter Harris, trans. William Marsden (New York, 2008), p. 291.

27 Arnved Nedkvitne, *Norse Greenland: Viking Peasants in the Arctic* (London, 2018), p. 35.

28 Robert McGhee, *The Last Imaginary Place: A Human History of the Arctic World* (Ottawa, 2004), pp. 97–8.

29 Ingvar Svanberg, 'A Russian Polar Bear in Stockholm: Notes on Animal Diplomacy', *Svenska Linnésällskapets årsskrift = Yearbook of the Swedish Linnaeus Society* (2016), p. 113.

30 Barbara Ravelhofer, '"Beasts of Recreacion": Henslowe's White Bears', *English Literary Renaissance*, XXXII/2 (Spring 2002), p. 294.

31 McGhee, *Last Imaginary Place*, p. 100.

32 Oleson, 'Polar Bears', p. 50.

33 Jacques Cartier, *Jacques Cartier and his Four Voyages to Canada*, trans. Hiram B. Stephens (Montreal, 1890), p. 13.

34 Ibid.

35 Frank Jones, *Life of Martin Frobisher, Knight* (London, 1878), p. 138.

36 Gerrit de Veer, *The Three Voyages of William Barents to the Arctic Regions in 1594, 1595, and 1596*, 2nd edn, ed. Charles T. Beke and Koolemans Beynen (London, 1876), pp. 15–16.

37 Ibid., p. 171.
38 Ibid., pp. 62–4.
39 Louwrens Hacquebord, 'In Search of Het Behouden Huys:
    A Survey of the Remains of the House of Willem Barentsz on
    Novaya Zemlya', *Arctic*, xlviii/3 (September 1995), p. 255.
40 Ibid.
41 De Veer, *Three Voyages of William Barents*, p. 183.
42 C.C.A. Gosch, *Danish Arctic Expeditions, 1605 to 1620* (London,
    1897), pp. 24–5.
43 Huw W. G. Lewis-Jones, 'Nelson and the Bear: The Making of an
    Arctic Myth', *Polar Record*, 219 (2005), pp. 335–53.
44 Olaudah Equiano, *The Interesting Narrative of the Life of Olaudah
    Equiano, Or Gustavus Vassa, The African* (London, 1789), pp. 212–13.
45 Vincent Carretta, *Equiano the African: Biography of a Self-made Man*
    (Athens, GA, 2005), p. 147.
46 See Dickenson, *Seal*, pp. 123–6.

2 IT'S A BEAR'S LIFE

1 Quoted in Dan Slavik, *Inuvialuit Knowledge of Nanuq: Community
   and Traditional Knowledge of Polar Bears in the Inuvialuit Settlement
   Region* (2009), p. 27.
2 Stuart Houston, Tim Ball and Mary Houston, *Eighteenth-century
   Naturalists of Hudson Bay* (Montreal, 2003), p. 1.
3 Pliny the Elder, *Pliny's Natural History*, trans. Philemon Holland
   (London, 1847–8), p. 63.
4 'COSEWIC Assessment and Update Status Report on the Polar Bear
   Ursus Maritimus in Canada', www.registrelep-sararegistry.gc.ca,
   accessed 26 February 2018.
5 See, for example, the 1766 image by Peter Mazell in Nat Williams,
   'Chasing the Polar Bear: Images of Polar Bears across Time', www.
   nla.gov.au, 13 May 2015.
6 Georges-Louis Leclerc, Comte de Buffon, *Natural History: General
   and Particular* (Edinburgh, 1780–85), part 8, www.quod.lib.umich.
   edu, accessed 26 February 2018.

7 Gaston R. Demarée and Astrid E. J. Ogilvie, 'The Moravian Missionaries at the Labrador Coast and their Centuries-long Contribution to Instrumental Meteorological Observations', *Climate Change*, XCI/3–4 (2008), pp. 423–50; Hans J. Rollman, 'Christian Gottlob Barth and the Moravian Inuktitut Book Culture of Labrador', *Newfoundland and Labrador Studies*, XXXII/2 (2017), p. 404.

8 Victor P. Lytwyn, *Muskekowuck Athinuwick: Original People of the Great Swampy Land* (Winnipeg, 2002), p. 110.

9 Samuel Hearne, *A Journey from Prince of Wales's Fort in Hudson's Bay to the Northern Ocean* (London, 1795), p. 270.

10 Charles Darwin, *On the Origin of Species by Means of Natural Selection* (London, 1859), p. 184.

11 James Lamont, *Seasons with the Sea Horses, or Sporting Adventures in the Northern Seas* (London, 1861), pp. 273–5.

12 Ibid., p. 277.

13 C. Leah Devlin, 'The Letters between James Lamont and Charles Darwin on Arctic Fauna', *Polar Record*, 51 (2015), pp. 497–8.

14 Robert E. Bieder, *Bear* (London, 2005), pp. 9–10.

15 See Don E. Wilson and DeeAnn M. Reeder, eds, *Mammal Species of the World: A Taxonomic and Geographic Reference*, 3rd edn (Baltimore, MD, 2005), www.press.jhu.edu, accessed 26 February 2018.

16 Jennifer S. Holland, 'New Video Shows that Returning Pandas to the Wild Actually Works', www.news.nationalgeographic.com, 19 April 2017.

17 Ragnhild Nordahl Næss, 'The Finnøy Polar Bear', www.phys.org, 23 January 2018.

18 See C. R. Harington, 'The Evolution of Arctic Marine Mammals', *Ecological Applications*, XVIII/2 (2008), pp. S23–S40.

19 S. Liu et al., 'Population Genomics Reveal Recent Speciation and Rapid Evolutionary Adaptation in Polar Bears', *Cell*, CLVII/4 (2014), pp. 785–94.

20 Charlotte Lindqvist et al., 'Complete Mitochondrial Genome of a
   Pleistocene Jawbone Unveils the Origin of Polar Bear', *Proceedings
   of the National Academy of Sciences, USA*, CVII/11 (2010), pp. 5053–7.

21 Liu et al., 'Population Genomics', p. 787.

22 Jodie D. Pongracz et al., 'Recent Hybridization between a Polar
   Bear and Grizzly Bears in the Canadian Arctic', *Arctic*, LXX/2
   (June 2017), pp. 151–60.

23 James A. Cahill et al., 'Genomic Evidence of Geographically
   Widespread Effect of Gene Flow from Polar Bears to Brown Bears',
   Molecular Ecology, XXIV (2015), pp. 1205–17.

24 Ian Stirling, *Polar Bears: The Natural History of a Threatened Species*
   (Markham, ON, 2011), p. 94.

25 Ibid., pp. 97–9.

26 J. P. Whiteman et al., 'Summer Declines in Activity and Body
   Temperature Offer Polar Bears Limited Energy', *Science*,
   CCCXLIX/6245 (17 July 2015), pp. 295–8.

27 N. K. Advani, *Polar Bear*, WWF Wildlife and Climate Change Series
   (Washington, DC, 2016).

28 Sharon Chester, *The Arctic Guide: Wildlife of the Far North*
   (Princeton, NJ, 2016), p. 98.

29 The International Arctic Buoy programme monitors air
   temperature and ice movement; see http://iabp.apl.washington.
   edu, accessed 18 February 2018.

30 'Clever Polar Bear Stalks Seal', *Polar Bear: Spy On The Ice, Preview*,
   BBC One, www.youtube.com, 22 December 2010.

31 Stirling, *Polar Bears*, p. 194.

32 Ibid., p. 278.

33 See Richard H. Russell, 'The Food Habits of Polar Bears
   of James Bay and Southwest Hudson Bay in Summer and
   Autumn', *Arctic*, XXVIII/2 (1975), pp. 117–29.

34 Linda J. Gormezano and Robert F. Rockwell, 'What to
   Eat Now? Shifts in Polar Bear Diet during the Ice-free Season

in Western Hudson Bay', *Ecology and Evolution*, III/10 (2013), pp. 3509–23.

35 Michelle Theall, 'Alaska Whale Hunt Keeps Polar Bears Alive', www.sierraclub.org, 9 June 2018.

36 K. L. Laidre et al., 'Historical and Potential Future Importance of Large Whales as Food for Polar Bears', *Frontiers in Ecology and Environment* (9 October 2018).

37 A. M. Pagano et al., 'High-energy, High-fat Lifestyle Challenges an Arctic Apex Predator, The Polar Bear', *Science*, CCCLIX/6375 (2 February 2018), pp. 568–72.

38 See 'Polar Bear POV Cam', www.youtube.com, 2016, accessed 20 February 2018.

39 Nikita Ovsyanikov, *Polar Bears: Living with the White Bear* (Vancouver, 1996), p. 81.

40 Ron R. Togunov, Andrew E. Durocher and Nicholas J. Lunn, 'Windscapes and Olfactory Foraging in a Large Carnivore', *Scientific Reports*, www.nature.com, 12 April 2017.

41 Frédéric Laugrand and Jarich Oosten, *Hunters, Predators and Prey: Inuit Perceptions of Animals* (New York, 2015), pp. 184–6.

42 Thomas G. Smith et al., 'A Review of the Developmental, Behavioural and Physiological Adaptations of the Ringed Seal, *Phoca Hispida*, to Life in the Arctic Water', *Life in the Polar Winter*, XLIV/2 (June 1991), pp. 124–31.

43 Quoted in P.D.N. Herbert and J. Wearing Wilde, eds, *Igloolik Oral History Project, Canada's Polar Life* (2002), www.polarlife.ca, accessed 28 February 2018.

44 Quoted in 'Nanuq', in *Canada's Polar Life*, ed. P.D.N. Herbert and J. Wearing Wilde (2002), www.polarlife.ca, accessed 19 February 2018.

45 Sarah Benson-Amram et al., 'Brain Size Predicts Problem-solving Ability in Mammalian Carnivores', *Proceedings of the National Academy of Sciences of the United States of America*, CXIII/9 (2016), p. 2532.

46 Stirling, *Polar Bears*, p. 206.

47 Ibid., pp. 208–11.

48 Ibid., p. 105.

49 Matilda Brindle and Christopher Opie, 'Postcopulatory
Sexual Selection Influences Baculum Evolution in
Primates and Carnivores', *Proceedings of the Royal Society
B, Biological Sciences*, CCLXXXIII/1844 (14 December 2016),
http://rspb.royalsocietypublishing.org, accessed 13 February 2018.

50 Stirling, *Polar Bears*, p. 112.

51 Ibid., p. 42.

52 Ibid., p. 126.

53 Ibid., p. 127.

54 Ibid., p. 42.

55 Ibid., p. 118.

56 Ibid., p. 112.

57 Ibid., pp. 96–7.

58 Daniel W. Koon, 'Power of the Polar Myth', *New Scientist*,
CLVIII/2131 (25 April 1998), p. 50.

59 'A High-tech Way to Count Polar Bears', www.arctic.blogs.panda.
org, 9 May 2016.

60 John Bennett and Susan Rowley, eds, *Uqalurait: An Oral History
of Nunavut* (Montreal, 2004), p. 292.

61 George M. Durner et al., 'Consequences of Long-distance
Swimming and Travel over Deep-water Pack Ice for a Female
Polar Bear during a Year of Extreme Sea Ice Retreat', *Polar Biology*,
XXXIV/7 (July 2011), pp. 975–84.

62 Bruce Barcott, 'Polar Bear Cubs Drowning due to Sea Ice Loss,
Says Report', www.theguardian.com, 19 July 2011.

63 Eric V. Regehr et al., 'Integrated Population Modeling Provides
the First Empirical Estimates of Vital Rates and Abundance for
Polar Bears in the Chukchi Sea', *Scientific Reports*,
www.nature.com, 14 November 2018.

64 'Satellite Collars', https://polarbearsinternational.org, accessed 23 February 2018.

65 Megan Hamilton, 'Polar Bear Collars, Tranquilizers Don't Do Lasting Harm', www.digitaljournal.com, 1 March 2018.

66 Steve Amstrup and Trent McDonald, 'Mark-recapture', http://pbsg.npolar.no, accessed 14 February 2018.

67 Kelly McSweeney, 'Intel's Falcon 8+ Drone Launched from Research Boats despite Steel Interference', *Robotics* (6 October 2017); Seth Stapleton et al., 'Polar Bears from Space: Assessing Satellite Imagery as a Tool to Track Arctic Wildlife', www.journals.plos.org, 9 July 2014.

68 Wendle, 'See How They Track'.

69 U.S. Fish and Wildlife Service, *Polar Bear Annual Report 2016*, www.fws.gov, 1 March 2018.

70 Paul Nadasdy, 'The Gift of the Animal: The Ontology of Hunting and Human-Animal Sociality', *American Ethnologist*, XXXIV/1 (2007), p. 37.

3 ARCTIC SPECTACLE

1 Herman Melville, *Moby-Dick*, ed. Mary R. Reichart (San Francisco, CA, 2011), p. 238.

2 Russell A. Potter, *Arctic Spectacles: The Frozen North in Visual Culture, 1818–1875* (Seattle, WA, 2007), pp. 10–11.

3 Francis Spufford, *I May Be Some Time: Ice and the English Imagination* (London, 1996), plate 9.

4 Joseph Conrad, *Heart of Darkness*, 2nd edn, ed. D.C.R.A. Goonetilleke (Peterborough, ON, 1999), pp. 66–7.

5 Ursula Le Guin, 'Sur', in Le Guin, *The Compass Rose* (New York, 1982), pp. 343–84.

6 Rinie van Meurs and John F. Splettstoesser, 'Farthest North Polar Bear (Ursus maritimus)', *Arctic*, LVI/3 (2003), pp. 308–9.

7 For that story see Wally Herbert, *The Noose of Laurels* (New York, 1989).

8 Matthew Henson, *A Negro Explorer at the North Pole* (New York, 1912), p. 72.

9 Bruce Henderson, 'Who Discovered the Pole?', www.smithsonianmag.com, April 2009.

10 Quoted ibid.

11 Quoted in Anna Marshall, 'Gustave Doré's Images for *The Ancient Mariner*: Style and Controversy', *Victorian Visual Culture*, http://qub.ac.uk, accessed 18 February 2018.

12 Mary Shelley, *Frankenstein*, ed. D. L. Macdonald and Kathleen Scherf (Peterborough, ON, 1999), p. 49.

13 Ibid., p. 50.

14 [John Barrow], 'Ross's Voyage of Discovery', *Quarterly Review*, 21 (1819), p. 252.

15 Ibid., p. 222.

16 Robin Jarvis, *Romantic Readers and Transatlantic Travel: Expeditions and Tours in North America, 1760 to 1840* (Burlington, VT, 2012), pp. 113–14.

17 This was not a joke; see, for just one example, Kenn Harper's *Minik: The New York Eskimo: An Arctic Explorer, a Museum, and the Betrayal of the Inuit People* (2017) for the story of Inuit who were brought to New York by Robert Peary. Minik's father died, the museum staged a fake burial to deceive Minik and then put his father's skeleton on display.

18 'The Illustrating Traveller: Encountering Native Americans', http://brbl-archive.library.yale.edu, 4 September 1996.

19 Spufford, *I May Be Some Time*, p. 51.

20 Coll Thrush, 'The Iceberg and the Cathedral: Encounter, Entanglement and Isuma in Inuit London', *Journal of British Studies*, LIII (January 2014), p. 65.

21 Edmund Burke, *On the Sublime and Beautiful*, xxiv, Pt 2 (New York, 1909–14), www.bartleby.com, accessed 19 February 2018.

22 Potter, *Arctic Spectacles*, p. 43.

23 Spufford, *I May be Some Time*, p. 51.

24 Andrew Moore, 'Sir Edwin Landseer's "Man Proposes, God Disposes": And the Fate of Franklin', *British Art Journal*, IX/3 (Spring 2009), p. 327.

25 For more on this story, see David C. Woodman's *Unravelling the Franklin Mystery: Inuit Testimony*, 2nd edn (Montreal, 2015) and John Walker's documentary, *Passage* (2008).

26 Arthur Conan Doyle, *Life on a Greenland Whaler: An Account of Doyle's Seven-month Voyage as a Surgeon on the Whaler 'Hope' in 1880*, www.gutenberg.net.au, accessed 12 June 2018.

27 Kathryn Schulz, 'Literature's Arctic Obsession', www.newyorker.com, 24 April 2017.

28 W. G. Burn Murdoch, *Modern Whaling and Bear-hunting: A Record of Present-day Whaling with Up-to-date Appliances in Many Parts of the World, and of Bear and Seal Hunting in the Arctic Regions* (London, 1917), p. 197.

29 Ibid., p. 276.

30 Ibid., p. 267.

31 Ibid., p. 304.

32 Ibid., pp. 303–4.

33 James Hogg, 'The Surpassing Adventures of Allan Gordon', ed. Gillian Hughes, *Altrive Chapbooks*, II/1 (1987), www.english.stir.ac.uk, accessed 15 December 2017.

34 Victoria Dickenson, *Seal* (London, 2016), pp. 95–104.

35 Hogg, 'The Surpassing Adventures of Allan Gordon'.

36 Ibid.

37 Peter Christen Asbjørnsen, 'King Valemon, the White Bear', in *Tales from the Fjeld: A Series of Popular Tales* (New York, 1917), pp. 376–88; 'East of the Sun and West of the Moon', in *East of the*

Sun and West of the Moon: Old Tales from the North (New York, 1914), pp. 9–27.

38 Franz Boas, *The Central Eskimo* (Lincoln, NE, 1964), pp. 230–31.

4 ENTERTAINING POLAR BEARS

1 Geoff Ryman, *The Child Garden* (Easthampton, MA, 1989), p. 30.

2 Quoted Barbara Ravelhofer, '"Beasts of Recreacion": Henslowe's White Bears', *English Literary Renaissance*, XXXII/2 (Spring 2002), p. 309; this article should be credited with the detailed information about Henslowe's polar bears in this chapter.

3 'Shakespeare's Competition: The Grisly World of British Bear-baiting', www.theconversation.com, 19 April 2016.

4 Ben Jonson, 'The Induction', *Bartholomew Fair* (London, 1910), p. 182.

5 'The Crazy Christmas When 70 Polar Bears Descended on Leicester Square', www.londonist.com, 4 December 2017.

6 Coll Thrush, 'The Iceberg and the Cathedral: Encounter, Entanglement and Isuma in Inuit London', *Journal of British Studies*, LIII/1 (January 2014), p. 64.

7 Quoted Harmut Lutz et al., ed. and trans., *The Diary of Abraham Ulrikab: Text and Context* (Ottawa, 2005), p. 16.

8 Ibid., p. 5.

9 Nigel Rothfels, *Savages and Beasts: The Birth of the Modern Zoo* (Baltimore, MD, 2002), p. 199.

10 Ibid., p. 202.

11 Frances L. Beers, 'To a Silver King', *New York Times* (19 July 1914), p. SM6.

12 Ros Clubb and Georgia Mason, 'Animal Welfare: Captivity Effects on Wide-ranging Carnivores', *Nature*, CDXXV/6957 (2003), pp. 473–4.

13 William T. Hornaday, *Popular Official Guide to the New York Zoological Park* (New York, 1915), p. 121.

14 'Countries with Restrictions or Ban of Wild Animals in Circuses', 19 June 2018, www.four-paws.org, accessed 8 December 2018.

15 Colin Fernandez, 'Caged Animals Forced to Perform at Heythorp Zoo in Oxfordshire', www.dailymail.co.uk, 17 January 2016.

16 Edward Struzik, *Arctic Icons: How the Town of Churchill Learned to Love its Polar Bears* (Markham, ON, 2014), p. 197.

17 'The Suarez Troupe', www.circopedia.org, accessed 10 June 2018.

18 Hornaday, *Popular Official Guide to the New York Zoological Park*, p. 119.

19 'A New Home for Britain's Last Polar Bear', www.telegraph.co.uk, 17 December 2009.

20 N. R. Kleinfield, 'Farewell to Gus, Whose Issues Made Him a Star', www.nytimes.com, 28 August 2013. Una Chaudhuri describes Deke Weaver's performance based on Gus in 'The Silence of the Polar Bear: Performing (Climate) Change in the Theatre of the Species', *Readings in Performance and Ecology*, ed. Wendy Arons and Theresa J. May (New York, 2012), pp. 45–57; Reuven Blau, 'Bronx Zoo's Beloved Tundra – The Last Polar Bear in NYC – Dies at 26', www.nydailynews.com, 28 December 2017.

21 The Tragically Hip, *In Between Evolution* (2004), track 4.

22 Marcel Chotkowski LaFollette, *Science on American Television* (Chicago, IL, 2014), p. 47.

23 'Conservation Potential', www.waza.org, accessed 5 March 2018.

24 Born Free, Introduction, 'EU Zoo Inquiry, 2011', www. euzooinquiry.eu, accessed 14 February 2018.

25 Amy Corrigan, 'An Investigation into the Welfare of Captive Polar Bears in Japan', www.zoocheck.com, accessed 19 February 2018.

26 Echo Huang, 'The World's Saddest Polar Bear is Just One of Thousands of Arctic Animals Living in Malls in China', https://qz.com, 22 September 2016.

27 'See All 70 Polar Bears in North American Zoos', www.oregonlive. com/data/2017/10/polar_bear_census.html, 2 November 2017.

28　The BBC has several videos of polar bears testing remote-controlled spy cameras to destruction, see www.youtube.com.

29　Jason Burke, 'Knut's a Millionaire Bear, While He's Cuddly', www.theguardian.com, 12 May 2007.

30　Else Poulsen, *Bärle's Story: One Polar Bear's Amazing Recovery from Life as a Circus Act* (Vancouver, 2014), p. 192.

31　Noel R. F. Snyder et al., 'Limitations of Captive Breeding in Endangered Species Recovery', *Conservation Biology*, x/2 (April 1996), p. 344.

32　Ibid., p. 346.

33　Gail Hedberg, 'Polar Bears', in *Hand-rearing Wild and Domestic Mammals*, ed. Laurie J. Gage (Oxford, 2002), p. 181.

34　Juliet Eilperin, 'Captivity Could Help Polar Bears Survive Global Warming Assault, Some Zoos Say', www.washingtonpost.com, 25 March 2012.

35　Manitoba, Wildlife Branch, Species Monitoring, 'Polar Bears in Manitoba', www.gov.mb.ca, accessed 19 February 2018.

36　'"Enough's Enough": Number of Polar Bear Cubs Shipped Out of Churchill Could be Cut Back', www.cbc.ca, 5 December 2017.

37　Lucy Byatt, Bryndís Snæbjörnsdóttir and Mark Wilson, Introduction, *nanoq: flat out and bluesome: A Cultural Life of Polar Bears* (London, 2006), p. 16.

38　See www.1stdibs.com.

39　Leopold Sacher-Masoch, *Venus in Furs*, trans. Fernanda Savage (London, 1921), www.gutenberg.com, accessed 19 February 2018.

40　This is an anonymous rhyme satirizing Glyn's bestselling novel *Three Weeks* (1907), in which the 'Tiger Queen' writhes seductively on a tiger skin.

41　Evelyn Waugh, *Men at Arms* (London, 1952), p. 152.

42　See Paula Uruburu, *American Eve: Evelyn Nesbit, Stanford White, the Birth of the 'It' Girl, and the Crime of the Century* (New York, 2009).

43 Ed Caesar, 'Rupert Bear Gets a 21st Century Makeover',
www.independent.co.uk, 3 March 2018.

44 Sianne Ngai, 'The Cuteness of the Avant-garde', *Critical Inquiry*,
XXXI/4 (2005), pp. 819, 828.

45 Ibid., p. 816.

5 IT TAKES TWO TO TANGLE

1 Quoted in Dan Slavik, *Inuvialuit Knowledge of Nanuq: Community
and Traditional Knowledge of Polar Bears in the Inuvialuit Settlement
Region* (North Slope, AK, 2010), p. 9.

2 Edward Struzik, *Arctic Icons: How the Town of Churchill Learned
to Love its Polar Bears* (Markham, ON, 2014), p. 22.

3 Martyn Gorman, 'The Slaughter of the Whales', 2002,
www.scran.ac.uk, accessed 18 February 2018. The bowhead is
the only whale of commercial interest that stays in the Arctic
year-round. For the impact of whalers on Inuit communities,
see Dorothy Harley Eber, *When the Whalers Were Up North: Inuit
Memories from the Eastern Arctic* (Montreal, 1989).

4 Alexander Starbuck, *History of the American Whale Fishery from
its Earliest Inception to the Year 1876* (Waltham, MA, 1878), p. 100.

5 Ian Stirling, *Polar Bears: The Natural History of a Threatened Species*
(Markham, ON, 2011), p. 247.

6 James Emerson Honderich, 'Wildlife as a Hazardous Resource:
An Analysis of the Interaction of Polar Bears and Humans in
the Canadian Arctic, 2000 BC to 1935', MA thesis, University
of Waterloo, Canada, 1991, abstract.

7 Stirling, *Polar Bears*, p. 249.

8 Michael Engelhard, *Ice Bear: The Cultural History of an Arctic Icon*
(Seattle, WA, 2017), p. 4.

9 Quoted in Kieran Mulvaney, 'Polar Bear Attacks Surprisingly Rare',
www.seeker.com, 5 August 2011.

10 James M. Wilder et al., 'Polar Bear Attacks on Humans: Implications of a Changing Climate', *Wildlife Society Bulletin*, XLI/3 (2017), abstract.

11 Thomas Pennant, *Synopsis of Quadrupeds* (London, 1771), p. 194.

12 Georges-Louis Leclerc, Comte de Buffon, *Natural History: General and Particular* (Edinburgh, 1780–85), part 8, pp. 220–21.

13 James Hogg, 'The Surpassing Adventures of Allan Gordon', ed. Gillian Hughes, *Altrive Chapbooks*, II/1 (1987), www.english.stir.ac.uk, accessed 15 December 2017.

14 Oliver Goldsmith, *A History of the Earth, and Animated Nature* [1774] (Glasgow, 1840), vol. I, p. 550.

15 Struzik, *Arctic Icons*, p. 20.

16 Erin E. A. Ross, '"Hey, lay off my carcass!" Grizzlies Chase Polar Bears Away from Important Food Source', www.sciencemag.org, 8 December 2015.

17 'Sergey Ananov, Russian Pilot Rescued in Arctic, Recounts 2-day Ordeal', www.cbc.ca, 27 July 2015.

18 Nikita Ovsyanikov, *Polar Bears: Living with the White Bear* (Vancouver, 1996), p. 45.

19 Engelhard, *Ice Bear*, pp. 136–7.

20 Else Poulsen, *Smiling Bears: A Zookeeper Explores the Behavior and Emotional Life of Bears* (Vancouver, 2009), p. 67.

21 Jon Mooallem, *Wild Ones: A Sometimes Dismaying, Weirdly Reassuring Story About Looking at People Looking at Animals in America* (New York, 2013), p. 29.

22 Ibid.

23 Peter Benchley, 'Great White Sharks', *National Geographic* (April 2000), p. 12.

24 'The Polar Bear Family and Me,' www.youtube.com, accessed 1 March 2018; this video played on BBC Two in 2013, and has had 4.2 million views on YouTube.

25 List of Fatal Bear Attacks in North America, www.en.wikipedia. org, accessed 5 March 2018.

26 *Agreement on the Conservation of Polar Bears*, www.pbsg.npolar.no, 15 November 1973.

27 See www.feedingnunavut.com.

28 Quoted in Slavik, *Inuvialuit Knowledge of Nanuq*, p. 11.

29 Quoted in Nancy Wachowich, with Apphia Agalakti Awa, Rhoda Kaukjak Katsak and Sandra Pikujak Katsak, *Saqiyuq: Stories from the Lives of Three Inuit Women* (Montreal, 1999), p. 78.

30 Fikret Berkes, *Sacred Ecology*, 2nd edn (New York, 2012), p. 98.

31 Darren Keith et al., *Inuit qaujimaningit nanurnut = Inuit Knowledge of Polar Bears: A Project of the Gjoa Haven Hunters' and Trappers' Organization* (Gjoa Haven, NU, 2005), p. 73.

32 Frédéric Laugrand and Jarich Oosten, *Hunters, Predators and Prey: Inuit Perceptions of Animals* (New York, 2015), p. 9.

33 Quoted ibid., p. 34.

34 Quoted ibid., p. 41.

35 Keavy Martin, *Stories in a New Skin: Approaches to Inuit Literature* (Winnipeg, 2012), pp. 47–58.

36 Zebedee Nungak and Eugene Arima, *Eskimo Stories: Unkkaatuat* (Ottawa, 1969), p. 67.

37 Stirling, *Polar Bears*, p. 51.

38 Robert J. Flaherty, 'How I Filmed *Nanook of the North*', www.documentary.org, accessed 25 February 2018. The film can be seen at the 'Nanook of the North' entry on Wikipedia, https://en.wikipedia.org, accessed 20 February 2019.

39 Dean W. Duncan, 'Nanook of the North', www.criterion.com, 12 January 1999. Robert J. Christopher, *Robert and Frances Flaherty: A Documentary Life, 1883–1922* (Montreal and Kingston, 2005), p. 403.

40 Quoted in Slavik, *Inuvialuit Knowledge of Nanuq*, p. 6.

41 Marina Tyrrell, 'West Hudson Bay Polar Bears: The Inuit Perspective', *Inuit, Polar Bears and Sustainable Use: Local, National, and International Perspectives*, ed. Milton M. R. Freeman and Lee Foote (Edmonton, 2009), p. 105.

42 Stirling, *Polar Bears*, pp. 51–4.

43 Quoted in Slavik, *Inuvialuit Knowledge of Nanuq*, p. 10.

44 Nunavut, Wildlife Management Division, *Summary of Hunting Regulations 2018–19*, www.nu.ca, accessed 21 February 2019.

45 Sara Frizzell, 'Inuit Lives Must Be Protected over Polar Bears, Nunavut Community Says', www.cbc.ca, 14 November 2018.

46 'Economic Importance', www.polarbearscanada.ca, accessed 10 February 2018.

47 Dan Slavik, 'The Economics and Client Opinions of Polar Bear Conservation Hunting in the Northwest Territories, Canada', in *Inuit Polar Bears and Sustainable Use: Local, National, and International Perspectives*, ed. Milton M. R. Freeman and Lee Foote (Edmonton, 2009), p. 72.

48 Quoted in Slavik, *Inuvialuit Knowledge of Nanuq*, p. 24.

49 See www.bearskin-rugs.com, accessed 10 February 2018; see also CITES Scientific Authority, 'Polar Bear: Non-detriment Finding', www.canada.ca, 30 June 2017.

50 See the website of the Polar Bear Specialist Group of the IUCN, http://pbsg.npolar.no.

51 For more on debates around hunting quotas, see Gloria Dickie, 'As Polar Bear Attacks Increase in Warming Arctic, a Search for Solutions', 19 December 2018, https://e360.yale.edu/features.

52 Eric V. Regehr et al., 'Harvesting Wildlife Affected by Climate Change: A Modelling and Management Approach for Polar Bears', *Journal of Applied Ecology*, LIV/5 (8 March 2017), pp. 1534–43.

53 CITES Scientific Authority, 'Polar Bear: Non-detriment Finding'.

54 Slavik, *Inuvialuit Knowledge of Nanuq*, p. 20.

55 'Polar Bear Non-invasive Sampling Methods', www.north-slope. org, accessed 1 March 2018; see C. D. Brower et al., 'The Polar Bear Management Agreement for the Southern Beaufort Sea: An Evaluation of the First Ten Years of a Unique Conservation Agreement', *Arctic*, LV/4 (2002), pp. 362–72.

56 Tyrrell, 'West Hudson Bay Polar Bears' pp. 105–6.

57 Wendy Donner, 'Animal Rights and Native Hunters: A Critical Analysis of Wenzel's Defence', *Canadian Issues in Environmental Ethics* (Peterborough, ON, 1997), p. 162.

58 George W. Wenzel, *Animal Rights, Human Rights: Ecology, Economy and Ideology in the Canadian Arctic* (Toronto, 1991), pp. 7–8.

59 Tanya Tagaq, 'Tanya Tagaq: Polaris Music Prize Winner', www.cbc.CA, 26 September 2014.

60 Franz Boas, *The Central Eskimo* (Lincoln, NB, 1964), p. 101.

61 Nuligak, *I Nuligak*, ed. and trans. Maurice Metayer and Olive Koyama (New York, 1971), p. 110.

62 Roger Frison-Roche, *Hunters of the Arctic*, trans. Len Ortzen (Toronto, 1974), p. 237.

63 Susan McHugh, '"A Flash Point in Inuit Memories": Endangered Knowledges in the Mountie Sled Dog Massacre', *English Studies in Canada*, XXXIX/1 (2013), pp. 149–75.

64 *Qikiqtani Truth Commission: Community Histories 1950–1975* and *Qikiqtani Truth Commission: Thematic Reports and Special Studies* (Iqaluit, 2010), www.qtcommission.ca, accessed 18 June 2018.

65 George Wenzel, 'Inuit and Polar Bears: Cultural Observations from a Hunt near Resolute Bay, N.W.T.', *Arctic*, XXXIV/1 (1983), p. 94.

66 Stirling, *Polar Bears*, pp. 238–42.

67 Hampton Sides, 'Russian Refuge', www.nationalgeographic.com, May 2013.

68 'Lunch Arrives on Wrangel Island', www.siberiantimes.com, 29 September 2017.

69 Damien Sharkov, 'Take a Tour of Russia's Giant New Military Base', www.newsweek.com, 18 April 2017.

70 Struzik, *Arctic Icons*, p. 43. Mutanen was just one of 117 relocated Dene who died in Churchill as a result of poor conditions there.

Many Dene moved back to their homeland, to Tadoule Lake in 1973. Eventually they received an apology and compensation from Manitoba (2010) and the federal government (2016).

71 Struzik, *Arctic Icons*, p. 102.

72 Brent Wlock, Manitoba Conservation Officer, oral communication, 2 November 2017.

73 'Polar Bears in Manitoba', www.gov.mb.ca, accessed 19 February 2018.

74 Wlock, oral communication.

6 SAVE THE POLAR BEARS!

1 Yuko Tawada, *Memoirs of a Polar Bear*, trans. Susan Bernofsky (New York, 2014), p. 210.

2 Brandon Kerfoot, 'Claiming Animals, Claiming Sovereignty: Animal Welfare, Indigeneity, and Sovereignty in the Canadian Eastern Arctic', PhD dissertation, University of Alberta, 2018.

3 Ian Stirling, rev. of *Ice Bear*, by Michael Engelhard, *Arctic*, LXX/3 (September 2017), p. 330.

4 Spencer Weart, *The Discovery of Global Warming*, https://history.aip.org, January 2017.

5 *Time* magazine, http://content.time.com, 3 April 2006.

6 *Vanity Fair*, www.vanityfair.com, 1 May 2007; Knut, too young and valuable to travel, was photoshopped into the frame.

7 Larry Greenemeier, 'U.S. Protects Polar Bears Under Endangered Species Act', www.scientificamerican.com, 14 May 2008.

8 Weart, *The Discovery of Global Warming*.

9 Yale Program on Climate Change Communication, Yale Climate Opinion Maps, 2016-US, www.climatecommunication.yale.edu, accessed 10 February 2018.

10 Pew Research Center, 'Global Concern about Climate Change, Broad Support for Limiting Emissions', www.pewresearch.org, 5 November 2015.

11 Netherlands Environmental Assessment Agency, *Trends in Global CO_2 Emissions*, 2016 Report (The Hague, 2016), pp. 38, 40.

12 Susan J. Crockford, www.polarbearscience.com, 21 November 2015.

13 Stirling, *Polar Bears*, p. 196.

14 'Ursus maritimus', www.iucnredlist.org, accessed 27 February 2018.

15 *Effects of Climate Change on Polar Bears: Fact Sheet*, www.worldwildlife.org, accessed 9 January 2018.

16 Crockford, www.polarbearscience.com, 26 July 2012.

17 Ibid., 5 November 2017; 11 December 2017.

18 J. Aars, N. J. Lunn and A. E. Derocher, *Polar Bears: Proceedings of the 14th Working Meeting of the IUCN/SSC Polar Bear Specialist Group, Seattle, Washington, 20–24 June 2005*, Occasional Paper of the IUCN Species Survival Commission 32 (Gland, Switzerland, 2006), p. 61; S. C. Amstrup, B. G. Marcot and D. C. Douglas, 'Forecasting the Rangewide Status of Polar Bears at Selected Times in the 21st Century', U.S. Geological Survey (Reston, VA, 2007).

19 Steven Amstrup, quoted in Erica Goode, 'Climate Change Denialists Say Polar Bears Are Fine. Scientists Are Pushing Back', www.nytimes.com, 10 April 2018.

20 Jeffrey A. Harvey et al., 'Internet Blogs, Polar bears, and Climate-change Denial by Proxy', www.academic-oup.com, 29 November 2017.

21 Suzanne Goldenberg, 'Leak Exposes how Heartland Institute Works to Undermine Climate Science', www.theguardian.com, 15 February 2012.

22 Crockford, www.polarbearscience.com, 15 January 2018.

23 See IUCN/SSC Polar Bear Specialist Group population status reviews for Beaufort Sea, Western Hudson Bay, and Southern Hudson Bay, www.pbsg.npolar.no, accessed 20 January 2019.

24 Crockford, 'Testing the Hypothesis that Routine Sea Ice Coverage of 3–5 mkm^2 Results in a Greater than 30% Decline in Population Size of Polar Bears (*Ursus Maritimus*)', *Peer J Preprints*, www.peerJ.inc, 2 March 2017.

25 Cristina G. Mittermeier, 'Starving-polar-bear Photographer Recalls What Went Wrong', www.nationalgeographic.com, August 2018.

26 Ibid.

27   See Andrew Stuhl, *Unfreezing the Arctic: Science, Colonialism, and the Transformation of Inuit Lands* (Chicago, IL, 2016).

28   Edward Struzik, *Arctic Icons: How the Town of Churchill Learned to Love its Polar Bears* (Markham, ON, 2014), p. 5.

29   See the Commission on the Comprehensive Test-ban Treaty, www.ctbto.org, for histories of these tests.

30   Garrett Hinchey, 'Arctic Cruise Ship Owners Ordered to Pay $469K in Costs for 2010 Grounding', www.cbc.ca, 9 February 2017. The *Clipper Adventurer*, with 197 aboard, struck a rock shelf near Kugluktuk, Nunavut, in 2010. Those responsible were judged negligent and fined for the costs of remediating the spill of pollutants. More recently, a Russian-flagged ship, *Akademik Ioffe*, ran aground in Nunavut with 162 aboard on 24 August 2018, fortunately with no loss of life or pollutant spill.

31   Kate Lunau, 'Why Does Canada Still Allow Hunters to Kill Polar Bears for their Fur?', http://motherboard.vice.com, 4 May 2016.

32   Quoted in Dan Slavik, *Inuvialuit Knowledge of Nanuq: Community and Traditional Knowledge of Polar Bears in the Inuvialuit Settlement Region* (North Slope, AK, 2010), p. 28.

33   Quoted ibid., p. 29.

34   Ibid.; see also Zacharias Kunuk and Ian Mauro, *Inuit Knowledge and Climate Change*, 2010, www.isuma.tv, accessed 14 February 2018.

35   Some scientific papers rely on data collected by Inuit hunters and recorded in the past, such as this study of polar bears in dens, which could not be carried out today as disturbing occupied dens is illegal. Franz Van de Velde, Ian Stirling and Evan Richardson, 'Polar Bear (*Ursus maritimus*) Denning in the Area of the Simpson Peninsula', *Arctic*, LVI/2 (2003), pp. 191–7.

36   'Tallurutiup Imanga: A Final Boundary for Canada's Largest Protected Area at Lancaster Sound in Nunavut', www.pc.gc.ca, accessed 21 February 2018.

37   Daniel V. W. Slavik, 'Knowing Naunut: Bankslanders Knowledge and Indicators of Polar Bear Population Health', MSc thesis, University of Alberta, 2013, p. 173.

38 Paul Nadasdy, 'The Gift of the Animal: The Ontology of Hunting and Human-Animal Sociality', *American Ethnologist*, XXXIV/1 (2007), p. 37.

39 Bianca Nogrady, 'Can Business Save the World from Climate Change?', www.greenbiz.com, 5 September 2017.

40 'Last Ice Area', www.worldwildlife.org, accessed 21 February 2018.

41 Damien Sharkov, 'Take a Tour of Russia's Giant New Military Base', www.newsweek.com, 18 April 2017.

42 Sophie Paradis, 'Polar Bear on Thin Ice', www.blog.wwf.ca, 18 November 2015.

43 David Harradine, 'It's the Skin You're Living In', www.feveredsleep. co.uk, accessed 21 February 2018.

44 Many issues of *The Economist*, to which I subscribe and which I read with great interest.

Select Bibliography

Berkes, Fikret, *Sacred Ecology*, 2nd edn (New York, 2012)

Betts, Matthew W., Mari Hardenberg and Ian Stirling, 'How Animals Create Human History: Relational Ecology and the Dorset-Polar Bear Connection', *American Antiquity*, LXXX/1 (2015), pp. 89–112

Brandson, Lorraine E., *Churchill, Hudson Bay: A Guide to Natural and Cultural Heritage* (Churchill, MB, 2016)

Byers, Michael, *Who Owns the Arctic?: Understanding Sovereignty Disputes in the North* (Vancouver, 2010)

Chester, Sharon, *The Arctic Guide: Wildlife of the Far North* (Princeton, NJ, 2016)

Derocher, Andrew E., *Polar Bears: A Complete Guide to their Biology and Behaviour* (Baltimore, MD, 2012)

Ellis, Richard, *On Thin Ice: The Changing World of the Polar Bear* (New York, 2009)

Emberley, Julia V., *The Cultural Politics of Fur* (Ithaca, NY, 1997)

Engelhard, Michael, *Ice Bear: The Cultural History of an Arctic Icon* (Seattle, WA, 2017)

Grace, Sherrill, *Canada and the Idea of North* (Montreal, 2007)

Kolbert, Elizabeth, *The Sixth Extinction: An Unnatural History* (New York, 2014)

Laugrand, Frédéric, and Jarich Oosten, *Hunters, Predators and Prey: Inuit Perceptions of Animals* (New York, 2015)

Lewis-Jones, Huw W. G., 'Nelson and the Bear: The Making of an Arctic Myth', *Polar Record*, 219 (2005), pp. 335–53

Lopez, Barry, *Arctic Dreams* (New York, 1986)

McGhee, Robert, *The Last Imaginary Place: A Human History
of the Arctic World* (Ottawa, 2004)

Martin, Keavy, *Stories in a New Skin: Approaches to Inuit Literature*
(Winnipeg, 2012)

Oceans North Conservation Society, World Wildlife Fund Canada,
and Ducks Unlimited Canada, *Canada's Arctic Marine Atlas*,
www.oceansnorth.org, accessed 28 February 2019

Ovsyanikov, Nikita, *Polar Bears: Living with the White Bear*
(Vancouver, 1996)

Poulsen, Else, *Smiling Bears: A Zookeeper Explores the Behavior and
Emotional Life of Bears* (Vancouver, 2009)

—, *Bärle's Story: One Polar Bear's Amazing Recovery from Life as a Circus
Act* (Vancouver, 2014)

Ravelhofer, Barbara, '"Beasts of Recreacion": Henslowe's White Bears',
English Literary Renaissance, XXXII/2 (Spring 2002), pp. 287–323

Stirling, Ian, *Polar Bears: The Natural History of a Threatened Species*
(Markham, ON, 2011)

Struzik, Edward, *Arctic Icons: How the Town of Churchill Learned to Love
its Polar Bears* (Markham, ON, 2014)

Tawada, Yoko, *Memoirs of a Polar Bear*, trans. Susan Bernofsky
(New York, 2014)

Ulrikab, Abraham, *The Diary of Abraham Ulrikab: Text and Context*,
ed. and trans. Hartmut Lutz et al. (Ottawa, 2005)

Watt-Cloutier, Sheila, *The Right to be Cold: One Woman's Story
of Protecting her Culture, the Arctic, and the Whole Planet*
(Toronto, 2015)

FILMOGRAPHY

Donohue, Shannon, and Frank Tyro, directors, *Walking Bear Comes
Home: The Life and Work of Chuck Jonkel A Pioneer of Bear Biology*,
a Great Bear Foundation and Caribou Crossing Production (2017)

Kunuk, Zacharias, and Ian Mauro, dir., *Inuit Knowledge and Climate
Change* (2010), www.isuma.tv

Associations and Websites

ALASKA SCIENCE CENTER
www.alaska.usgs.gov
Managed by the u.s. Geological Survey, the centre conducts research into polar bears and provides a list of articles on the subject.

THE ARCTIC INSTITUTE
www.thearcticinstitute.org
The website of the Center for Circumpolar Security Studies founded in 2011. An independent non-profit policy and research organization based in Washington, DC, which 'strives to move beyond common conceptions of the Arctic as a uniform and remote region'.

BEARS IN MIND
www.bearalert.org
A Dutch foundation that works on public education about bears, mainly in Europe, and maintains a website on which people can post information about zoo bears that appear to be abused.

CAFF: CONSERVATION OF ARCTIC FLORA AND FAUNA
www.caff.is
CAFF is the biodiversity working group of the Arctic Council (www.arctic-council.org), a high-level intergovernmental organization of the eight countries with territory within the Arctic Circle: Canada, Denmark, Finland, Iceland, Norway, Russia, Sweden and the United States.

ENVIRONMENT AND CLIMATE CHANGE, CANADA

www.ec.gc.ca

Provides maps of ice coverage, including an animation for ice formation over the past ten days. Particularly useful for obsessing over ice formation in Hudson Bay and the Beaufort Sea in October, when the polar bears are waiting hopefully for the ice to form so they can go hunting.

EYE ON THE ARCTIC

www.rcinet.ca

Initiated and co-ordinated by Radio Canada International, the site is supported by media in Canada, Finland, Norway, Sweden and the u.s. 'to better tell the stories of communities and people directly affected by climate change'. The full spectrum of news reporting from an Arctic perspective, including the latest on polar bears.

GREAT BEAR FOUNDATION

www.greatbear.org

A non-profit organization founded in 1981 'dedicated to the conservation of the eight species of bears and their habitat around the world'. It runs educational programmes about polar bears in Churchill, Manitoba.

IUCN POLAR BEAR SPECIALIST GROUP

www.pbsg.npolar.no

Provides a great deal of scientific information about polar bears, including detailed information on polar bear numbers for each of the nineteen subpopulations, including maps. It also provides complete texts of important agreements that deal with polar bears. The FAQ page is useful for a general audience.

IUCN RED LIST OF THREATENED SPECIES

www.iucnredlist.org

Explains the reasons for the listing of polar bears as 'vulnerable'. Provides a detailed and thorough account of threats, range and other information about polar bears.

THE OREGONIAN/OREGONLIVE

www.projects.oregonlive.com/data/2017/10/polar_bear_census.html
Interactive map with tiny biographies for all seventy polar bears in accredited zoos in Canada and the U.S., updated October 2017.

POLAR BEARS INTERNATIONAL

https://polarbearsinternational.org
A non-profit polar bear conservation organization that supports polar bear research and education. PBI maintains polar bear cams in Churchill and regularly produces educational videos. Their informative website even allows you to hear the various sounds polar bears make, from chuffing to humming.

THE POLAR BEAR PROGRAMME (RUSSIA)

http://programmes.putin.kremlin.ru
Vladimir Putin 'is actively involved in the protection of rare animals and personally oversees the programmes on Amur tigers, polar bears and white whales'. Provides a Russian take on the history of polar bear research, upcoming projects, and many pictures of Putin with polar bears.

SCOTT POLAR RESEARCH INSTITUTE, CAMBRIDGE UNIVERSITY

www.spri.cam.ac.uk
The institute was founded in 1920 to honour Captain Robert Falcon Scott and his four companions at the pole. It conducts research on the polar and cold regions of the world.

U.S. FISH AND WILDLIFE SERVICE, MARINE MAMMALS MANAGEMENT, ALASKA

www.fws.gov
The U.S. agency responsible for the conservation of polar bears. The site includes plans, annual reports, agreements, training manuals and harvest quota information.

Acknowledgements

I would like to thank Hartmut Lutz for the image of Abraham Ulrikab; Nigel Rothfels for the poem by Frances Beers; Daniel Heath Justice for many picture suggestions and a convivial conference, Animalfest, where I first encountered many knowledgeable and fascinating Reaktion Books Animal series authors; June Scudeler, for inviting me to her class at Simon Fraser University when she was showing Alethea Arnaquq-Baril's NFB documentary, *Angry Inuk*; Ian Stirling for his helpful suggestions on polar bear biology and behaviour and the importance of science and local ecological knowledge working together for the conservation of polar bears; Hugo Voss, for creating a chart at the last minute; Jasmine Spencer, for commenting on the introduction; Brandon Kerfoot, for the sharp insights in his doctoral dissertation; Shannon Donohue and Frank Tyro of the Great Bear Foundation for their excellent guiding in Churchill and for introducing the group to the Manitoba Conservation Resource officers, particularly Brent Wlock; Churchill Northern Studies Research Centre for its educational programming; Lou Parsons for good company on the trip; Keavy Martin for pointing me to useful resources; Sneja Gunew for giving me Yuko Tawada's book; Victoria Dickenson for help with images and much else; the Reaktion team for useful editorial suggestions and help finding images; and all the friends and relations who listened patiently to me talking endlessly about polar bears. As always, I thank the Musqueam people for their hospitality on their unceded traditional territory.

All opinions and errors in the book are, of course, my responsibility.

Photo Acknowledgements

The author and publishers wish to express their thanks to the below sources of illustrative material and/or permission to reproduce it. Some locations of artworks are also given below, in the interests of brevity:

akg-images: p. 135; courtesy B&C Alexander/Arcticphoto: p. 160; courtesy Tim Anderson: p. 106; photo Steven Amstrup, USGS: p. 68; from Peter Christen Asbjørnsen, *East of the Sun and West of the Moon: Old Tales from the North* (New York, 1922): p. 99; The Art Institute of Chicago (open access): pp. 89, 140; from John James Audubon and John Bachman, *The Quadrupeds of North America*, vol. II (New York, 1851): p. 62; The British Library, London: p. 46; from Edward Brown, *An Account of Several Travels through a Great Part of Germany* (London, 1677), photo Wellcome Collection: p. 108; The Canadian Museum of History, Gatineau: pp. 26, 64; from Samuel Taylor Coleridge, *Der Alte Matrose* (Leipzig, 1877): p. 87; from James Cook, *A Voyage to the Pacific Ocean* (London, 1784), photo Wellcome Collection, London: p. 48; © DACS 2019/© Erbengemeinschaft Günter Schmitz/Sammlung Stiftung Stadtmuseum (Berlin VG Bild Kunst 982202/01): p. 119; photo Commander Eric Davis, NOAA Corps: p. 75; photo Terry Debruyne, USFWS: p. 138; from Olaudah Equiano, *The Interesting Narrative of the Life of Olaudah Equiano, or Gustavus Vassa, the African* (London, 1789): p. 43; photo Margery Fee: p. 162; Hamburger Kunsthalle, Hamburg: p. 93; © Her Majesty the Queen in Right of Canada, as represented by the Minister of the Environment, 2019: p. 19; photos Patrick Kelley, U.S. Coast Guard: pp. 167, 170; from *Kongl. Vitterhets Historie och Antiqvitets Akademiens Månadsblad* (Stockholm, 1872): p. 30; Kristin

Laidre/University of Washington: p. 95; from Georges-Louis Leclerc, Comte de Buffon, [*Collection des animaux quadrupèdes: planches coloriées sans texte*] (Paris, 1754), photo courtesy Bibliothèques universitaires de Strasbourg: p. 47; Library of Congress, Prints and Photographs Division, Washington, DC: pp. 20, 85, 102, 112, 114, 117, 132, 150; McCord Museum, Montreal (N-0000.68.1): p. 29; courtesy Moravian Archives, Herrnhut: p. 110; Musée des Beaux-Arts et d'Archéologie de Besançon: p. 25; Museum of Fine Arts, Boston (open access): p. 123; Nasjonalbiblioteket, Norway: pp. 38, 100, 130; National Gallery of Art, Washington, DC (open access): p. 63; Nordnorsk Kunstmuseum, Tromsø: p. 143; NWT Archives: pp. 149 (Archibald Fleming, N-1979-050-1168), 146 (Robert C. Knights, N-1993-002-0252); © Polar Bears International/polarbearsinternational.org: pp. 58, 105 (Simon Gee); from Johannes Isacius Pontanus, *Rerum et urbis Amstelodamensium historia* (Amsterdam, 1611): p. 39; private collection: pp. 59, 80; from *Punch, or the London Charivar* (June 5, 1875): p. 82; from John Ross, *Narrative of a Second Voyage in Search of a North-west Passage* (London, 1835), photo Biodiversity Heritage Library: p. 15; from John Ross, *A Voyage of Discovery* (London, 1819): p. 54; Royal Holloway, University of London: p. 92; from William Smith, *The Particular Description of England, 1588* (London, 1879): p. 104; Tate Britain, London: p. 10; The University of Texas at Austin, Perry-Castañeda Library Map Collection: p. 16; U.S. Navy photo by Chief Yeoman Alphonso Braggs: p. 84; courtesy Hugo Voss: p. 53; from Ole Worm, *Museum Wormianum, seu, Historia rerum rariorum* (Leiden, 1655), photo Biodiversity Heritage Library: p. 129.

Andrea & Stefan, the copyright holders of the image on p. 124; Emma Bishop, the copyright holder of the image on p. 163; Tony R. Brown, the copyright holder of the image on p. 76; Payton Chung, the copyright holder of the image on p. 178; Jean-Pierre Dalbéra, the copyright holder of the image on p. 28; GoToVan, the copyright holder of the image on p. 8; Christopher Michel, the copyright holder of the images on pp. 61 and 147; Anita Ritenour, the copyright holder of the image on p. 65; and Angell Williams, the copyright holder of the image on p. 71, have published them online under conditions imposed by a Creative Commons Attribution 2.0 Generic License. Stefan David, the copyright holder of the image on p. 56;

Index

Page numbers in *italics* refer to illustrations

Agreement on the Conservation of Polar Bears 11, 21, 56, 73, 103, 137, 145
Amundsen, Roald 378, *38*, 81, 111
anthropomorphism 10–11
Arctic, the 13–14, 17–18, 79–82, *82*, 86–7, 91, 94, 173
Attenborough, David 121
Audubon, John James, 'Polar Bear' *62*

Barentsz, Willem 38–40, *39*
Barrow, John, British Admiralty 88
BBC (British Broadcasting Corporation) 21–2, 121, 144
bear-baiting 103–7
bear spray 161
bears, species 52–3, *53*
    black bear (Kermode; *Ursus americanus*) 23, 49–50
    brown bear (also grizzly; *Ursus arctos*) 7–8, 23–4, *25*, 48–9, 52–3, 55–6, 70, 118
    cave bear (*Ursus spelaeus*) 24
    giant panda (*Ailuropoda melanoleuca*) 8, 35, 52, 54
    hybrid 55–6
    in children's literature 52, 117, 133
    see also bear-baiting; polar bear
Benchley, Peter, *Jaws* 144
Biard, François-Auguste, *Fight with Polar Bears 143*
Blake, William, *Newton 10*, 11, 165, 182
Boas, Franz 98, 156
Böttcher, Ursula 118–19, *119*, 124
Brontë, Charlotte 91
Buffon, Georges-Louis Leclerc, Comte de, 'The Polar Bear' *47*, 48–9, 140–41

captive breeding 54, 125–7
    see also Knut; zoos
cave art *see* pictographs
Churchill, Manitoba 12–13, 17, 49, 75, 137, 143–4, 160–62
    ice conditions 158–9
    polar bear management *162*, *163*, 163–4

circuses 21, 28–9, 103, 108–11, 115, 118, *119*
climate change 24, 27, 29, 35
 denial 167, 168–71
 global warming 21–2, 55–6, 123, 125, 127, 154, 165–8
Coleridge, Samuel Taylor, *Rime of the Ancient Mariner* 86, *87*
colonization 23, 35, 45, 80, 81, *82*, 155, 173
commercial use and commodification of polar bears 23, 44, 96, *106*, 108, 124–5, 133, *177*
 brands *102*, *134*, *135*
 see also fur trade; hunting of polar bears
Conrad, Joseph 81
Cruikshank, George, 88–9
 Landing the Treasures; or Results of the Polar Expedition 89
cruise ships 83, 123, 173–4

Darwin, Charles *50*, 51–2, 55, 92
dens
 polar bear 20–21, 49, 70–71, 159–60, 173
 ringed seal 60, 66–7, 80
DiCaprio, Leonardo 166
Dickens, Charles 88, 91, 92
dogs, sled and dogsleds (*qamutik*) 26, 38, 45, 84, 89, 151–2, *155*, 156–7
 see also bear-baiting
Doré, Gustave 86, *87*

Dorfinant, Gaston, *Buvez* Coca-Cola *135*
Dörflein, Thomas 124, *124*
Dorset people 23, 26–8
Doyle, Arthur Conan 93–4

Ehrenstrahl, David Klöcker 35
Equiano, Olaudah (Gustavus Vassa) 42–3, *43*
Endangered Species Act (U.S.) 152, 166, 169
exploration 45, 79–92, 142–3
 see also names of individual explorers

Faulkner, William, 'The Bear' 97
Flaherty, Robert J. *see Nanook of the North*
Franklin, Lady Jane 92
Franklin, Sir John 91–2
Friedrich, Caspar David 90
 The Sea of Ice 93, 166
Frobisher, Martin 37, 90
fur 72–3, 103, 131–2, 155
 see also pelts, polar bear; trousers, polar bear
fur trade 9, 45, 49, 137–9, 155
 see also commercial use and commodification of polar bears

Galschiøt, Jens 179–80
 Unbearable 180
genetic research 23, 55, 74–6, 103, 126–7

Global Seed Vault, Svalbard,
Norway *126*, 127
global warming *see* climate change
Godwin, Mary *see* Shelley, Mary
Goldsmith, Oliver 141
Gore, Al, *An Inconvenient Truth*
21–2, 168
greenhouse gas emissions *see*
climate change
Greenpeace 22, 137, 175, 176–8, *179*

Hagenbeck, Carl 108–12
Haste, Kendra, *Polar Bear 33*
Henslowe, Philip, 'Master of the
King's Beares' 105
Henson, Matthew 84–5, *85*
heroes and heroism *see* men,
representations of
Hogg, James, 'The Surpassing
Adventures of Allan Gordon'
96–8, 141
Howett, Samuel, 'Seamen on the
Whale Fishery Killing a Polar
Bear' *140*
Hudson's Bay Company *see* fur
trade
hunters, Inuit 14, *15*, 66–7, *67*, 149–
50, *150*, 151–2, 156–8, 174–5
see also Inuit people, beliefs
about animals; Nuligak
hunting of polar bears 21, 66, 77,
138–9, 145, 148, 152–8, 174–5
hybidization *see* bears, hybrid
ice 18, 36, 49, 66–7, 70, 90, 91,
151–3

drift ice *93*
hunting platform for polar
bears 51, 60–61, *61*, 62, 93–5,
95, 127, *159*
thin 74, 166, *167*, *170*, 169–72
see also Churchill, ice
conditions
International Union for the
Conservation of Nature *see*
IUCN
Inuit people
beliefs about animals 146–8,
151, 157–8
guides and translators for
explorers 85, 89
see also hunters, Inuit;
Traditional Ecological
Knowledge (TEK)
IUCN Red List of Endangered
Species 53, 122, 169, 171
IUCN Polar Bear Specialist Group
73, 153, 168, 175

Kakizaki, Hakyo, *Ininkari, Ainu
Chieftain of Akkeshi 25*
Kittelsen, Theodor, *White Bear
King Valemon 101*
Knut, zoo polar bear 123–5, *124*,
166

Lamont, James 24, 51–2
Landseer, Edwin Henry, 91–2
Man Proposes, God Disposes 92
Le Guin, Ursula, 'Sur', 83
Linnaeus, Carl 45, 48

Maréchal, Nicholas, *Ursus Maritimus 27*
meat 40–41, 43, 75, 145–6, 153, 156–7, 161
Medieval Warm Period *see* climate change
men, representations of 11–12, 41–2, *42*, 89, 92, 96–8, 143, *143*
menageries 33–4, 103, *107*, 108, *108* *see also* zoos
Meyerheim, Paul Friedrich, *Travelling Menagerie 107*
monarchs *see* rulers
Moravian missionaries 49, 111 *see also* Ulrikab, Abraham
Morris, Desmond 121
Munk, Jens 40–41
Murdoch, W.G. Burn 94–6
museums 88–9, 103, 128–9, *129*
Mutanen, Tommy, Sayisi Dene 161–2

Nanook of the North, film 149–51, *150*
Nappaaluk, Mitiarjuk 142
National Geographic Magazine 143–4, 172–3
Nelson, Horatio 41–2, *42*
Nesbit, Evelyn *132*, 133
Nielsen, Kay 99
Norse people 11, 23, 28–32, 35, *35*
North Pole 36, 81–3
Northeast Passage 38–40
Northwest Passage 14, 36, 38, 84, 88, 90, 91

nuclear testing 173
numbers of polar bears 73–4, 76, 122, 137, 153–4, 156, 169–72, 174 *see also* polar bears, counting; hunting of polar bears
Nuligak 156

oil and gas production 77, 173, 177–9, *178*, *179*, *180*
Oliver, John, 'View of the Elector of Saxony's Bear-garden' *108*

Parry, William 88, 89–90
Peary, Robert 81, 84–6
Pennant, Thomas 140
pelts, polar bear 31, 36, 95, 137–8, 145, *146*, 153
rugs 11–12, 32, *59*, 103, 131–3, *132*, 153 *see also* fur
Phipps, Constantine 18, 41–3
pictographs 23–4
Pliny the Elder 46–7
polar bears
abilities 64, 66–7, 68, *72*, 73
animatronic 117, 178, *179*
attacks on humans 137, 139–45
counting of 74–6, 77
diet 8, 33, *47*, 49, 51–2, 54, 59–64, 72
food-conditioned *160*, 161–4
in fiction and folklore 96–9, *99*, *100*, 123–4, 136, 141
reproduction, pregnancy and

lactation 58, 69–70, 159
lifespan and mortality 68, 169
names for 18–21, 145
seal-hunting tactics 63, 66–7, 70, 93–5, 120, 126
subpopulations 18, 19
as symbol 7, 28, 36, 97, 101, 165
see also Churchill, Manitoba; circuses; dens; fur; numbers; pelts, polar bear; radio collars; rugs, polar bear; tranquillizing polar bears; zoos
Pompon, François 130
Polar Bear 131
Poulsen, Else 118–20, 125, 142–3
protection of polar bears
see Agreement on the Conservation of Polar Bears; hunting of polar bears
Pullman, Philip, The Golden Compass 117

radio collars, 73, 74, 76
Rainey, Paul J. 115, 116
Raleigh, Charles S., Law of the Wild 63
Rasmussen, Knut 84
Red List of Endangered Species see IUCN Red List of Endangered Species
rock art see pictographs
Ross, John 14, 15, 88–9
'A Polar Bear Plunges into the Sea' 142

rulers, hereditary, and polar bears 31–6, 105
see also bear-baiting
Ryman, Geoffrey, The Child Garden 136

Sackheouse, John 89, 89
Schmitz, Günter, Ursula Böttcher and Alaska 118
science, empiricist 10, 10–11, 45–6, 78, 174–5
scientists, polar bear field 65, 139, 141–2, 161, 165, 169, 170–71
Scott, Robert 38, 81
seals 146, 155
see also dens, ringed seal; polar bears, diet
shamanism 26, 26, 30, 30
Shelley, Mary, Frankenstein 86–8, 136
Sheouak, 'White Whales Startled by Polar Bear' 64
Skene, Andrew M., 'Head of a White Bear' 54

Tagaq, Tanya 155–6
Tawada, Yoko, Memoirs of a Polar Bear 123–4
Tenniel, John, 'Waiting to be Won, Queen of the Arctic' 82
Traditional Ecological Knowledge (TEK) 45, 175
tranquillizing polar bears 74–5, 75, 77, 161, 163, 163, 164

trousers, polar bear *67*, 145, 149,
    150
tourism *see* Churchill, Manitoba;
    cruise ships

Ulrikab, Abraham *110*, 111

walrus 65, *66*, 149
Wapusk National Park 173
Webber, John, 'A White Bear' *48*
Westall, Richard, *Nelson and the*
    Bear, 42
whales 63, *64*, 138, 141, 159–60
whaling 17, 21, 44, 64, 93–4, 95–6,
    137–8, *140*, 160
women, representations of 80–83,
    82, 85, 91, 97, 131–3, *132*, *134*,
    141
WWF (World Wide Fund for
    Nature, World Wildlife Fund)
    137, 175, 177, 179–80

zoos 21, 54, 56, *112*, 118–24, *125*,
    127, 144–5
    enclosures *56*, *109*, *114*, 114,
    115, *117*, *120*, 120–21
    'frozen' zoos (tissue banks)
    127
    'immersion' zoo 112–15
    justifications for 127–8
    Tierpark Hamburg 108–9, *109*
    see also Hagenbeck, Carl;
    Knut; menageries; Ulrikab,
    Abraham